For my father who lost his fa
choice and for all of those Malt
kindness. My special gratitude, however, must go to Antonia
Attard aka "The Ginger Lady" and Vladimir Pisani who helped
to stave off the hunger and provided the much needed
affection…

Once a Soldier…

November 2013

This account is based upon my honest recollections of the time and documents the first eighteen years of my eventful life. It must be stressed that it is a pure and honest reproduction of my feelings and conclusions during those dark days; rather than a story told with the benefit of hindsight, or the grown-up understanding of human nature. Inevitably, some memories, along with the pain, have faded, but I have in no way embellished my story and have deliberately not resorted to poetic licence in the telling of it. Where there was doubt, I have researched and consulted with family members who shared my experiences. Some events may have become slightly chronologically confused; an inevitable factor when writing about occurrences long since consigned to memory. There will be those – personally connected - who may be hurt by what I have written and while I can only assure them that to cause upset was never my intention; this was a chapter of my life which in order for me to move on, required exorcism. I have faithfully put the thoughts and feelings of my childhood into adult words and although some things can be explained in adulthood, the fact remains that these events did occur and regardless of the circumstances, the account within faithfully reflects the way I truly felt during those tumultuous times on the island of Malta.

VM Frost

London, August 2012

Other books by VM Frost
By Conscience Bound
Dead Or Alive In Purgatory

Prologue

At the dawning of the new day, the boy lay on his makeshift bed beneath the stone stairs that led to the first floor; where in the bathroom, his younger brother also lay; not on a bed, but in the bath, his slight body covered only with a thin blanket. The bathroom shared the first floor with two bedrooms and a kitchen. In the main bedroom at the front of the house, just to the right of the enclosed and ornate timber balcony, lay the boy's mother, shifting uncomfortably, her belly swollen with the certainty of a new life to come.

Another flight of sandstone steps ascended to the roof where pet rabbits drummed out a warning with their furry feet and Brenda the chicken scratched around her cage looking for errant kernels of maize. The roof was also home to Candy the cocker spaniel who clawed endlessly but with futility at the untreated tics breakfasting on her blood. Flights of pigeons, their wings clapping together as though in self applause at their own aerobatics, raced through the cloudless Mediterranean sky above the house of the boy, his brother, and their mother with her unborn child. Donkey-drawn carts laden with vegetables and offal from the local abattoir, trundled their weary way through the streets below, their drivers calling out gruffly to the housewives who in such days of austerity, had come to rely on the pigs trotters and even bovine heads from which to make a meal for their families. The boy's mother had become adept at making all manner of weird and wonderful concoctions from a pig's head and the clapped out refrigerator groaned under her efforts of pate and brawn making activities. The Kerosene man was also out and about early and with hoarse shouts of "KERO...SENE!" he splashed his greasy sweet smelling spirit into metal measuring cans before decanting it into the hotch potch of plastic containers, held by haggling housewives in need of fuel, with which to fill their *Aladdin* heaters and lamps to keep out the cold and darkness of the evening to come.

At the uninspiring church at the bottom of the boy's street, the faithful queued to be first into the incense-filled interior for the first mass of the day. The women, heads veiled in local lace, gossiped and fingered their golden crucifix necklaces, while the men, in groups, a suitably macho distance from the women, hawked and cleared their throats of the previous days' cheap tobacco while cursing and bemoaning the state of their countries' economy and lack of work. Surly children, unimpressed with having been woken hours before school, sulked and whined for their breakfasts and threw stones at stray dogs fighting for scraps among the overturned dustbins.

Beneath the stairs, the boy stirred, he'd grown used to the discomfort of his so-called bed, but had slept fitfully despite this. As he opened his eyes to take in the new day, his sense of smell was assailed by the harsh odour of *Jeyes Fluid*; it wasn't dissimilar to the smell of *Creosote*, the black liquid used to weather proof wooden fences in more temperate climes. In the boy's household, the fluid was used on a daily basis to wash the tiled floors, and like *Creosote*, it was also jet black, but marketed as a disinfectant. When the stuff was added to water, it became a milky grey colour - the boy's mother had told him that the fluid was poisonous. The smell was emanating from underneath the boy's bed; he'd put a bowl of the stinking stuff there the day before - you could have called it a cry for help – a signal of distress sent out in the hope that his mother would notice the bowl under his bed and ask him what it had been doing there. He'd planned to look suitably sad, before replying in a small voice, that he'd intended to drink the contents of the bowl. That revelation, he reasoned, would surely bring about some much craved sympathy and if he was lucky, a loving hug into the bargain. No, this outcome wasn't to be and a day later, it was still there, under his bed, un-noticed by anyone except him, stinking his rough bed space out and giving him a headache.

It was around five-thirty am; the same time as it always had been, when the man let himself into the house. His steel-shod shoes clattered down the long tiled hallway towards the stairs and the boy's bed, his cheap aftershave swirling in his wake. With a shout that he should "Get up!" followed by the threat of a soaking from a bucket of water if he dared tarry, the man stamped his way up the stone stairs to his next port of call;

which was the bathroom where the boy's brother lay stiff and bruised from another night in the bathtub. A sure indication to the boy downstairs as to whether his unfortunate brother had wet the "bed" during the night, would be the noise of the overhead shower being turned on, drenching the bath's occupant below. The sound of water would be followed by the cruel laughter of the man, and the muffled sobbing of the shivering bed-wetter. The man continued through the house and into the front bedroom where his English mistress - mother to the two boys, lay. There was a third and older brother, but he'd left the island the year before, returning to his native land, where, aged sixteen, he'd been left to fend for himself in the harsh and unfamiliar landscape that had been 1970's London. Entering the room, the man stooped over the bed and caressed the bump, which was soon to be his fourth - but illegitimate child. The boy's mother looked sleepily up at him and smiled. It had been scarcely five hours since they had last been together, but not content with having stolen another man's wife, he was determined to keep her, *Rapunzel*-like, in the house with the balcony. Just a few hours to climb into his true marital bed after patting his own sleeping children's heads; a couple of hours sleep next to his wife, then back to his mistress, lest she awake before his return; or worse still, awake from the nightmare of her incarceration, pack her meagre belongings and flee her open prison.

The object of waking the boy at such an hour had been to send him to join the queue of churchgoers just down the road to the place of worship known colloquially as *Ta'Lourdes* (Madonna of Lourdes) The church had officially been the parish church for the area since 1974 but its architecture did little to inspire and its ugly presence on an island of beautiful ecclesiastic buildings, hadn't exactly perpetuated the tradition of heavy adornment and majesty. It was no more than functional, bland and 1970's like in its construction. It appeared to be a poor relation to the main church in the village, built more out of need than glorification. Ironic really, that the man, who was husband to another and father of three children of his own – an adulterer in such a catholic country - would be so religious. Not that *he* attended church. Perhaps, the boy would later reflect; the man had vicariously lived a religious life through sending him off to church every bloody morning!

Scratching at the night's irritating crop of mosquito bites, the boy, bleary- eyed, focussed on the bare stone wall opposite. There, next to the meshed- over ventilator hole, high up among the blood splats of tormenting mosquitoes past, he saw the mottled grey body of a primeval looking gecko, its head akin to that of a miniature alligator. The lizard's flat motionless form hugged the grimy sandstone, tiny feet stuck Velcro-like to the wall. Reptiles such as these were commonplace in the boy's house and paying the creature scant regard, he reluctantly dragged himself out of bed. As far as the pungent *Jeyes Fluid* beneath him was concerned, he'd give it another day to see if his mum would notice his pathetic cry for help…

Trudging wearily down the street to the church, he took in its dreary façade and nondescript bell tower and feeling totally devoid of any religious feeling, he walked wearily inside. Choosing his customary seat right at the back of the church, the English boy sat among the old ladies with their paper fans, and went trough the motions. He obeyed the ritual of standing, kneeling and sitting, he endured the interminable hour of meaningless Latin, and when the service was finally over, he steadfastly ignored the collection plate as it did the rounds. It wasn't an act of meanness; but put money on the plate? If only he'd had something to donate – he didn't even own a pair of underpants for God's sake! It wouldn't be long though – possibly due to his forced regular attendance – before he was taken on as an altar boy-cum-bell ringer and he'd been able to join the priest on the altar plinth, from where, plucked from among the kneeling faithful, he could now smugly look down upon the veiled heads during the ritual of collection without feeling ashamed or inadequate.

Mass over, the boy returned to the house with the balcony where, before he'd be allowed to eat anything, he'd be made to fill a bucket with clear water and add the fluid which made it milky. Then, on hands and knees, he'd be compelled to wash the tiled floors with a floor cloth. The only pleasure he got from this task, had been the boyish fun of bracing his legs up against the wall and pushing himself forward in a slide, propelling him from one side of the room to the other aided by the wet greasy floor. After this, he'd be lucky to be fed a hunk of dry bread and perhaps a cup of tea before heading off to the local government school with his more privileged neighbours and a game of marbles outside the gates before the bell rang. The bell, when it did ring, would herald a day of being picked on by his form teacher; a staunch Labour Party supporter who'd revelled in making the English boy feel about as welcome as a fart in an astronaut's suit.

The year was 1973, the country - Malta. A tiny seventeen-by-nine mile strip of rock steeped in history in the middle of the Mediterranean sea; the islands had been governed by the left-leaning Labour Party under the leadership of Don Mintoff, aka the "Architect" This had been Mintoff's second term and second year in power and he presided over the removal of all so-called British colonial forces; ironically replacing them with Chinese and Libyan influences. Mintoff's government hadn't exactly created an atmosphere, which embraced the English boy, and hostility directed at him from his mother's lover, meant that he felt as though he were *persona non grata*, both at home, and within certain communities on the island. His feeling of isolation was perpetuated by the fact that he wasn't even able to use the surname of his birth: a name that in the eyes of his mother's new man, was synonymous with the boy's father. As a result, for the nest few years, he'd had to become accustomed to being addressed by his mother's maiden name instead. The boy was thirteen years old and he'd been in the country for six years - not all of which had been quite so wretched...

Part One

Chapter One
A Decent Enough Start
'The natives seem friendly...'

The boy breathed his first breath in the maternity ward of Stamford hospital. His father – a Royal Air Force Corporal, had been based at RAF Wittering on the Lincolnshire Cambridgeshire border at the time, and so Stamford was the nearest place for the second of his three sons to be born. His father-in-law, would in time-honoured tradition, later refer to his grandson; born just within the boundaries of Lincolnshire as a "Lincolnshire yellow belly" Many reasons for this nickname have been offered, chief among which include the most credible two. The first being that the men of the Royal North Lincolnshire Militia wore bright yellow waistcoats for ease of recognition on the battlefield, while the second – and more plausible - alludes to the mail coach that ran from Lincoln to either York or London. This coach had a yellow undercarriage and upon its arrival from Lincoln, the locals were said to call out 'Here comes the Lincolnshire Yellow belly!' As for his grandmother, she'd allegedly been reluctant to take her newborn grandchild into her arms and showing a breathtaking lack of tact, she'd exclaimed loudly: 'He's got ginger hair!'

As a second child, the boy with the red hair had learned from the mistakes of his older sibling and later, his younger brother. He'd soon discovered how to inveigle a way into his parent's affections and so get his own way. He also learned that the threat of telling tales on his brother meant that he could curry favour with him. This may have been the case, but his older and smarter brother sometimes engineered situations for which ginger boy would take the rap. These situations would be often resolved by the boys' mantra of "If you tell on me, I'll tell on you" culminating in "OK, if you don't tell on me I won't tell on you!" No such bargain however was struck on that fateful evening when son number one employed a piece of devastating theatre in order to coerce son number two into shitting the bed. The Great pooh debacle had gone something like this.

The boys shared a room and pretty much went to bed at the same time. As they lay in their darkened bedroom, older brother says to ginger brother:

'I bet you don't pooh the bed'

Always up for a challenge, younger brother retorts:

'I will if you do!'

Much straining later, older brother declares:

'I've done it'

Ginger brother may have been younger, but he wasn't going to commit himself without some kind of proof and accordingly asked for confirmation of the dastardly deed. Quick as a flash, brother number one reaches across in the darkness and hands ginger a wad of sodden toilet paper, which he'd been chewing since the agreement to pooh the bed had been struck. Taking hold of it, Ginger is impressed, and as arranged; not to be outdone, he proceeds to proudly curl one out. He never did know what had prompted his father come into the room, but when he did it was with ill-concealed suspicion, that 'd asked what the hell the stink was. Seizing his moment of triumph over the pretender, son number one triumphantly announced that ginger boy had "shit the bed!" The boy however, wasn't immediately daunted, and assuming that his snitching brother would surely take his share of the punishment, confidently retorted with a: "And so has he!" At this, conniving older brother produced his sodden toilet paper with a self-righteous flourish accompanied by the damning words "No I haven't!"

It hadn't been the first time that the younger boy had been duped either; there was the case of the fateful gymnastics display, which took place in a garage with exposed metal roof beams. The game on this occasion had been to see who could jump from a stool and grab the beam before swinging from it around ten feet above the concrete floor. They took turns doing this, with the stool being moved a few inches further away from the beam after each successful leap. Quickly forgetting the "pooh in the bed" incident, the boy had entrusted his brother with the incremental moving of the stool. After his go, not wanting to be outdone by his kid brother, the designer of the garage gymnastics, had somehow distracted Ginger and moved the stool an impossible distance away. Initially noting that the stool seemed a long way away, the boy, rankling under the accusation of being a scaredy-cat, had taken his go. The next thing he knew, he was being cradled in his mother's arms being force-fed sweet tea and nursing an egg on his forehead! A similar episode a few years later had involved a bet – instigated by his brother (who else!) that he couldn't climb to the top of a tree. To his credit, he'd scaled three quarters up the plum tree before losing his footing and tumbling to the stony ground below. During this adventure, he'd remained conscious but a fractured cheekbone had swelled his face to double its size making his left cheek visible without needing to resort to a mirror. Older brother had shown some remorse on this one and had escorted the dazed boy home, along the way exhorting him not to tell their mother that he had instigated the whole thing. This suited the boy just fine; not only had he now got one up on his brother – something to hold against him at a later date – but he was also about to be plied with maternal sympathy – oh, and more sweet tea!

The boy's life back then had been a series of moves. His father, an instrument technician, tended to be moved around the country from base to base every two years or so. At first, this had been of no consequence to the boy; each move an adventure, but as he'd grown older, moving so frequently had meant that he had felt like the new kid at school with every move. It had been difficult to put down roots and he'd had to learn fast how to deal with the school bullies ever on the look out for new victims. The red hair so reviled by his grandmother, hadn't helped his standing as the new boy at school. One place he had grown fond of was his father's posting to RAF Saint Athan, close to Cardiff in Wales. They'd had a large garden in which the boys would re-enact the cowboy films they'd been allowed to see at the old folk's home across the road. The boy's put-upon older brother had, upon parental orders, taken his annoying ginger sibling with him and had been rewarded with the usual constant stream of questions during the film – 'Is he a goodie? Which one's the baddie?…'

Life back in those salad days of youth had been good and unremarkable. The boys had run around doing the things kids did; bonfire nights, penny for the guy, illicit fireworks, playing with dog pooh and flicking it around with lollipop sticks, messing around in streams hunting for tadpoles, making tents out of blankets and clothes horses and cheeking the neighbours. Their dad had been a dab hand at making swords and daggers out of wood and decorating them with his soldering iron. He'd once made a magnificent bow and arrow set, with the arrows actually being shod with proper barbed tips made from metal. When it was ready, he'd proudly demonstrated it to the admiring boys. Pulling the bow to its full extent, the boy's father had let loose his first arrow. In his excitement, he'd failed to notice his eldest son, who in his eagerness to get a grandstand view of the marvellous weapon's capability, suddenly ran into the arrow's intended flight path. Realising at the point of release that his son was in the middle of his target area, he dropped the bow and rushed over to where the kid was writhing around on the grass - an arrow embedded in the side of his nose! Now it was Dad's turn to entreat with the boy's brother, promising him sweets, an increase in pocket money – whatever it took for Mum not to be given the full version of what had just happened!

Meanwhile, 3,600 miles from Cardiff in a country occupying the South-Western end of the Arabian Peninsula - then known as Aden - British rule, in place since 1839, was in its death throes. An insurgency against the British known as the Aden Emergency, began with a grenade attack by the communist's National Liberation Front (NLF), against the British High Commissioner on 10 December 1963, killing one person and injuring fifty. A state of emergency was declared and in 1964, Britain announced its intention to grant independence in 1968, but with the stipulation that the British military would remain in Aden. The security situation deteriorated as NLF and FLOSY (Front for the Liberation of Occupied South Yemen) vied for the upper hand. In January 1967, there were mass riots between the NLF and their rival FLOSY supporters in the old Arab quarter of Aden town. This conflict continued until mid February, despite the intervention of British troops. During the period there were as many attacks on the British troops by both sides as against each other, culminating in the destruction of an Aden Airlines DC3 plane in the air with no survivors. On 30 November 1967 the British finally pulled out, leaving Aden and the rest of the FSA under NLF control. The Royal Marines, who had been the first British troops to occupy Aden, were the last to leave - with the exception of a Royal Engineer detachment.

Two years before these tumultuous events in Aden, a third brother came along and the following year, the boy's father was posted with his squadron, to RAF Luqa in Malta. The family were to spend three years on the island, chosen by the British government as a convenient jump off point and airbase from which to service operations in Aden. Packing up their belongings into tea chests, the boy's family flew on a propeller driven aircraft to what ostensibly, was to be their new Mediterranean home for the next three years. Arriving at RAF Luqa, the boy's father embarrassed his wife – a former member of the Women's Royal Air Force by quipping that "The natives seemed friendly" Their first home – a temporary arrangement - was a block of flats in Pieta. A few minutes drive from the island's capital Valletta, Pieta roughly translated as the Virgin Mary mourning the death of Jesus. The flats were a stone's throw from an inlet, in which there was an old boathouse. The older boys immediately set out to explore their new surroundings while their mother unpacked the few things they'd brought with them, all lovingly stowed in the silver foil-lined tea chests that had been de-rigueur in the 1960's removals and house moving business. An inhabitant of one of the tea chests, had been the boy's beloved "Big Jim" Jim had been a giant bear, almost twice the size of the boy at the time, and he'd been Ginger's faithful companion since he'd been a toddler. Pulling the crumpled and well-travelled bear from the chest, the boy's mother had smiled when she'd remembered the Christmas morning when her redheaded, freckly son had awoken to find that Santa had left him a giant furry friend at the end of his bed. Dragging the huge cuddly bear excitedly into his parent's room, the boy had been completely overwhelmed by the bear's size and had immediately christened him "Big Jim" Carrying the well-loved bear into her son's new bedroom, she'd lovingly placed it onto his bed.

To the excited new arrivals, Pieta was a million miles away from Cardiff; and sniffing the warm briny air, the boys had wandered among the tethered, creaking boats, taking in the warm dusty atmosphere and dodging erratic drivers as they jockeyed their ancient but well-kept Fords, French Simcas, Triumphs, bone- shaking 1930's Thames buses, and gaily decorated lorries through the narrow streets. In the event, Pieta was to be no more than a temporary home and after a few weeks, the family moved to Fgura in the south of the island. This was a lot nearer to their father's workplace and close to the historic bastions built by the Grandmasters of the Knights of St John in the sixteenth century, before being expanded following the unsuccessful attempt of the Turks to invade the island in the Great Siege of 1565. Their new home – number 6 Raymond Flats – was spacious and airy and decorated in an art deco style right down to the crystal wall lamps. The other flats also housed service families including Pru, the cross-eyed wife of another airman, who made an appearance on the landing from time to time startling the boys with her unfortunate looks.

The boy's earliest recollections of those days, was that of his mother assembling her sons and going through a list of things that could be safely eaten in what amounted in her eyes, to a strange and foreign land of which she knew virtually nothing. She'd delivered her instructions at though a schoolteacher at a lectern, holding aloft those items of food that she'd deemed safe for the boys to eat. The fact that Malta was a civilised country, run in those days very much on par with her own country, hadn't put her off her stride. Ironically, one of the first experiences of local food that the boys experienced was the sight of a young Maltese boy opposite their apartments. Armed with a homemade catapult made from a naturally forked twig and lengths of rubber inner tube, the local kid had brought down a sparrow from the trees before proceeding to devour it raw! Needless to say, dead birds didn't feature on their mother's list of food – raw or otherwise. What the boys had witnessed wasn't entirely surprising, since twenty years after the second world war had ended, sections of Maltese society were still recovering from the devastation wreaked on the island by Hitler and Mussolini. Their homeland reduced to rubble, the gallant Maltese had literally been on the brink of total starvation, due in the main to the maritime convoys bearing vital supplies of food and fuel being sunk with monotonous regularity by not only the Luftwaffe, but nearer to home, the menace in the form of Italian E boats. After two years of continuous aerial attack, the dockyards on the beleaguered island had been blitzed out of operation, allowing Rommel's supply ships to cross to North Africa almost unopposed. By April 1942, Axis Commander-in-Chief Field Marshal Kesselring reported Malta neutralised. The island was facing starvation and unless at least a proportion of the Pedestal convoy could fight its way through, Malta would face surrender.

Central to the convoy and a focus of constant enemy attacks was the large American *Texaco*-owned tanker *Ohio*. Without her valuable cargo, neither Spitfires nor submarines could operate from Malta's bases; Rommel's supplies to North Africa would continue unhindered, and Churchill's plans to invade occupied Europe from the south would be abandoned. Such monumental issues had formed the background to the epic saga of Operation Pedestal, and the tanker *Ohio*. After three days and nights of continuous attacks by German and Italian submarines, E-boats, dive-bombers and torpedo planes, several naval vessels had been lost and only 5 of the 14 merchantmen still survived. The *Ohio* had received a bomb in the engine room and collected two crashed aircraft on her decks, but miraculously her crew had put out the fires; however, her rudder was jammed over and, without power, she was stopped in the water. Crowded with survivors from sinking merchant ships, three Royal Navy destroyers stayed with the stricken tanker, aiding and supporting her heroic efforts to reach port. With a destroyer lashed to each side to provide power, and a third roped to her stern giving steerage, the creaking waterlogged tanker, barely afloat, had limped into port on August 15. Crowds lined the harbour walls to give the crews a tumultuous hero's welcome. As late as the 1970's, poorer Maltese housewives joined the weekly ration queue outside the prison gates in Paola from where they would be issued flour, oil and sugar labelled "A gift from America"

The nearest the newly-arrived English boys had got to wartime Malta, was the junk yard at the top of their road in Fgura, which had been rammed with old military hardware. The kids had risked the snarling Alsatian guard dogs and by working out the length of the chains tethering them, they'd explored the young boy's heaven of old steel helmets, burned out hulks of military vehicles, wreaths of rusting barbed wire and seemingly endless snakes of ammunition belt links. When they weren't taking a chance with the guard dogs, the boys ran around with the older kids of military families and had been accepted into one particular gang run by a girl called Angela, after having passed the initiation test of showing their bare bottoms! Their lives, in comparison with that of the locals, could have been described as affluent: being driven around in their father's brand new Triumph Herald, and even employing a cleaner-cum-maid. The boy had been fascinated with the way that the maid had brewed tea using a teabag, an object never before seen by him. In those days, there was an element within the Maltese community that resented the presence of the British, particularly those connected with the military. This was understandable after the pounding that the country had suffered during the war; a war not of their making, but one which, due to the island's geographical position and British rule, had made the inhabitants unwilling participants. Such resentment manifested itself one day while the boy and his older brother were out walking and exploring their new home. Without warning a local man with a dog in tow cried out "English pigs!" before setting his dog on the children. The older boy was either quicker on his feet or else more attuned to the imminent danger; either way, it was the ginger kid who'd ran into an open field, and upon whom the fury of the dog was unleashed. Losing his footing as the animal closed in, he'd fallen to the dusty ground and curled instinctively into a defensive ball - but not before the snarling dog had taken a lump out of his inner thigh!

The attack on the boys may have been unprovoked on this occasion, but later, finding an expanse of freshly laid concrete, they'd decided to walk straight through it leaving footprints in what had been a proud crafts man's handy work. Just as before, the older boy had either been swifter of foot, or else he'd seen – and failed to warn Ginger – the man emerging from his house, cup of tea in hand. In the event, the cement layer had chased, caught, and grabbed hold of the English boy before he'd got twenty yards down the road. The understandably enraged man had pulled him by the ear until the transgressor had actually heard the appendage cracking! Another blow to Anglo/Maltese relations and the usual brotherly mantra of "If you don't tell on me I won't tell on you!"

It was decided that the boy's schooling on the island would be entrusted to Verdala School. This was in the main a military school catering for the children of naval and army parents. It was situated to the south east of Cospicua and within the Cottonera Lines. The Lines were one of the largest project of military architecture ever undertaken by the Knights of Malta and encircled the three old cities of Cospicua, Vittoriosa and Senglea. Designed in the first half of the seventeenth century, the original purpose of the Lines had been to protect the three cities and their landward fortification. The Cottonera Lines got their name from Grandmaster Nicolas Cottoner, and during the Second World War, they'd provided shelter to the local population from the German bombing onslaught.

The headmaster of Verdala, surveyed his young charges from a tower-like structure, which was known by the kids as the "control deck" Their physical and psychological needs were tended to by a kind elderly lady called Nurse Baker, dressed in a uniform of starched nursing regalia, who ran the school sick bay. It seemed that even all these miles from home, being a new boy again, was to be exacerbated by the fact that air force children were in the minority and all the other kids had made it plain that the children of airmen just weren't welcome. It was, after all a navy and army school and so it wasn't long before the boy began to be bullied. One particular morning, being cornered by a group of army kids, he'd snatched up a long metal bolt and holding it aloft, he'd kept them at bay until a teacher arrived to quell the mini-mob. Part of the school curriculum was to encourage the younger boys to join the Cubs, the older ones the Scouts, with the female equivalent being Brownies or Girl Guides. The two older boys were enrolled into the Cubs, but during a trip to the Malta's sister island, Gozo, they had misbehaved, in some way breaking some rule or another, and were summarily dismissed! Conspiracy theorists may have murmured about the boys not being of naval or army parentage, but given their problems with integrating, it would have been more accurate to say that they had been all round little shits!

The boy's life back then hadn't all been educational misery though, and half of his two shillings-and-sixpence pocket money, was ritually spent at the Astra Cinema on his dad's airbase where he'd watched cowboy films and Flash Gordon while drinking Coke infused with Refresher sweets. Of course, this was no consolation to his older brother, who with the irritating ginger kid in tow, had had to put up with the obligatory inane questions about goodies and baddies! Weekends were spent exploring the rocks at Saint Thomas Bay on the south of the island, or at Mellieha Bay in the north. The latter was one of the few sandy beaches on the island, and walking barefoot down the road to the water, the bare soles of the boy's soft English feet had sunk into tarmac melted by the midday sun; burning them, and making it necessary to walk in a curious skipping kind of way, punctuated with "oohs" and "ahs" Equipped with fishing nets made from his mother's old tights, he'd scrambled among the rocks looking for some unfortunate creature to haul from the sanctity of its briny rock pool. Soft drinks for the boys and beers for the adults were kept cool inside a nylon string bag lowered into the crystal clear waters of the Mediterranean, and sandwiches made gritty by the sand and filled with mushy tomatoes and cheese, were devoured without a care. Once home, the boy's fair English skin, burned under the cloudless sky, would be red as a lobster - sun cream had been the domain of the more enlightened, and his body had acclimatised the hard way. In any case, the eventual result of peeling skin had served as a game between the boys and become a competition of who could peel the biggest unbroken sheet of dead skin from their bodies!

The boy's relationship with his mother had been close; back at Raymond Flats, he'd made a habit of sneaking into the marital bedroom and climbing into his parent's bed in the early hours of the morning. The minute he'd heard the door close on his dad going off to work on the mighty cold war English Electric Lightning jets, he'd sneaked in for a cuddle. Once there, he'd clamour for the well-worn story of the bear that loved *Fry's Chocolate Cream*. There, warm and cosy in his mother's arms, he'd never tire of the bear story. Related in a deep bear-like voice, the basic story had always been along the lines of a bear pleading to be fed the *Fry's Chocolate Cream*, so irresistible to him – and of course, this particular chocolate bar had been on her list of foods "safe to eat!"

The boy's parents social life was bubbling along nicely and on several nights a week, they'd sneak out of the house leaving the television on to simulate their continued presence, leaving the kids feigning sleep in their bedroom. It wasn't long before the older boy cottoned on to this after creeping along the corridor and pressing his ear to the sitting room door. Emboldened by the absence of voices other than those of the TV, he'd pushed open the door to find the room unoccupied. Excitedly summoning Ginger, the two had swigged the bitter tasting dregs from the locally brewed *Hop Leaf* pale ale from the bottles littering the table, before settling down to watch an illicit late night programme on the telly. Left to their own devices, the boys had begun to experiment with more than just dregs of beer - with matches and the magic of fire entering the arena of play. One night while alone in the house, Ginger's older brother had produced a box of matches, and while in the bathroom, they'd experimented with setting light to toilet paper. During this, a net curtain, billowing in the night breeze had caught alight. Luckily for the boys and the other occupants of Raymond Flats, the location of their experiment had provided a ready source of water, and panicking like crazy, they'd taken it in turns to fill a soap dish and it's lid with water, eventually extinguishing the fire. Pulling down the charred remnants of net curtain and hiding it under the rubbish in the bin, they'd sheepishly retired back to the safety of their bedroom with a "If you tell on me I'll tell on you!"

Unbeknown to the adventurous boys back at Raymond Flats, their mother and father had begun to widen their social circle from that of the close-knit military scene on the base, to that of local bars. Among the new friends they'd made was a quirky little guy known as Joe "The Magician" who when later introduced to the boys, had delighted them by pulling coins seemingly from mid-air, before giving them away. Another was a man who was to shape the rest of their lives…

Dark, handsome, sharply dressed and a successful businessman with links to influential politicians, the man had captivated the boy's mother and it hadn't been long before she'd begun to share not only the front seat of his flashy American Chevrolet Rambler, but increasingly stolen moments together while the boy's father was away on operations. The man was an agent for a Dutch electronics company that specialised in TV and radio sets that he imported and sold on their behalf from his shop on Hamrun High Street. Extremely talented when it came to the workings of TV sets, the man also carried out repairs in his shop. The only problem with regard to his relationship with the boy's mother was the fact that a few streets away from his shop lived his wife and three children. By any standards, these facts presented flies in ointment, but with Malta being a staunchly Roman Catholic country with no divorce laws, the situation was toxic to say the least. Of course the boy's were oblivious to the dark facts; they just knew that every now and then a big old American car (by now an immense and beautiful 1959 Chevrolet Impala, and known to the local police as the "aircraft carrier") would draw up outside the flats and they'd jump in it along with their mum and speed off to the nearest beach, leaving cross-eyed Pru twitching her curtains in their wake. There was chocolate, money and gifts along with an encouragement from mum that they refer to the man as "Uncle"

Naturally, as the boy's mother fell for the man, her feelings towards her husband began to cool. It had been a fairly gradual transition and the first the kids had known about it was the bickering, door slamming and raised voices from the living room. At one point, in a frustrated rage, the spurned husband had punched his hand through the glass panel of a door. Hearing the commotion, the boy had wandered into the hallway to see his father covered in blood and shouting: 'Now look what you've made me do!' Frayed tempers led to reckless acts and when one day the boy cheeked his stressed mother one time too many, she'd hurled the jar of food she had been about to open, onto the tiled floor where it smashed into a hundred pieces at the boy's bare feet. One of the larger jagged shards had hit the ginger kid's foot, opening up a deep two-inch gash and instantly staining the glass- strewn kitchen floor with his blood. Panicking and instantly full of remorse, the boy's mother had scooped him up in her arms and rushed downstairs and into the street, where as luck would have it, her husband was just driving down the road. Bundling him into the car, he was driven to his father's airbase where a medic – not known for his skill with a needle and thread – had stitched him up leaving a ragged dogleg of a scar. Despite retaining a sullen and hurt look throughout the proceedings, Ginger had lapped up the attention and milked his mother's contrition for all he'd been worth.

By the time the boy's fathers' three year posting to Malta had come to an end, his wife, still in thrall to the man with the Chevy Impala, had made the decision to leave her husband and remain on the island with her children. The family were to return to Britain together, parting company (ostensibly) forever once through the airport arrivals hall. The boy's enduring memory of these times was that of his father's face as he sat across from them; wordless and stony faced, on the aircraft taking him and his soon to be lost family, back to England. Through no fault of his own, he'd lost out to his suave love rival, and all the perceived trappings of success. As the aeroplane had taken him further away from the island where three years previously "The natives had seemed friendly" and closer to a life without his children; he hadn't had it within him to spare the boy's feelings - the ginger kid with the freckly face, who'd innocently had no inkling of what had gone wrong back on that dusty island…

Chapter Two
Starting To Go Downhill
'Like bloody cardboard...'

Touching down on the cold windswept runway of Royal Air Force Lyneham, the boys, used to three long Mediterranean summers, shivered, as with inquisitive brown faces pressed up against the tiny rain streaked Plexiglas windows, they watched the Wiltshire countryside whizz past. Their young memories were all but devoid of what English countryside looked like - particularly after Malta, with its barren landscape and scarcity of trees. Of course, had the boys been old enough to have had an interest in Maltese geographical history, they would have understood the reason for the lack of greenery in what had briefly been their adopted home.

Between 5000 BC and 1636, visitors and conquerors alike, had all contributed to the gradual deforestation of Malta. Sicilian farmers and shepherds cut the wood for farming, and the builders of temples had built their roofs with olive wood, Judas wood and ash. Later in the Bronze Age, pine trees were burned to melt bronze and the arrival of the Phoenicians, Carthaginians and Romans had all but destroyed the remaining forests, with the invaders stripping them in order to build their war galleys. There had been a brief respite when in 870, the Arabs imported citrus trees; but carried away what was left of the Judas trees. In the sixteenth century, the latest owners of the island; the Knights of Saint John, cut down around 50000 olive trees for cotton, prompting a report by the Order stating that "Malta is an island without trees" During the Great siege of 1565, the invading Turks cut what few trees remained using the wood for cooking and the demolition of bastions held by the knights. It had been Grandmaster Lascaris who'd begun the reforestation of the islands in 1636 when he planted a wood; not so much out of concern for the islands, but mainly so that his knights would have somewhere to hunt. As far as the boy's father had been concerned, if you had spoken of trees and the country's history, he probably would have retorted that he didn't give a damn about the island that had visited such misery on him. He may have also added that he hoped there had been just enough wood left to make a bonfire out of, upon which to toss the man who'd stolen his wife. In years to come, the boy couldn't remember leaving the aircraft, walking into the arrivals lounge or parting from his Dad. Couldn't remember whether he'd hugged him or even said goodbye. Once out of the airport, the boys and their mum had travelled to Swindon railway station from where they would begin their journey to the Midlands and a temporary stay with their maternal grandparents. They arrived at Swindon in the middle of a dark rainy night and dressed in their inadequate clothes, they'd shivered the night away on the deserted platform, until they had been able to board the first train of the day.

Number 54, Lawfred Avenue, Wednesfield in Wolverhampton - home to the boy's grandparents, had been the birthplace of his older brother and was where the newly created one parent family were now heading. Lawfred Avenue bounded a grassed area, known locally as "The Patch' and was home to a corner shop at one end, owned by a Pakistani man, and Hilda's shop at the other (Hilda would later amaze the boys with her bizarre appetite for raw sausages). Moving temporarily into number 54, the boys made themselves at home. Ginger's older brother reacquainted himself with his grandparents while the younger boys; who had no real memory of them up until now, began to familiarise themselves with the ways of their mother's parents. The boy had a bit of a head start, having spent time with his grandma on her annual jaunts to Malta. She'd arrive dressed in faux fur, dripping with costume jewellery and bearing gifts. Wearing her *Dame Edna* spectacles, she'd invariably arrive waft through airport arrivals carrying enough duty free *John Player Special* cigarettes to last the visit. Coming in cylindrical plastic containers of fifty, she'd scarcely been seen without one of them hanging from her lips, long ash succumbing to gravity and falling where she stood – or in the case of when she did the washing up – in the sink! When she visited, grandma had been a regular at the Lucky Bar, hanging out with Joe The Magician's crowd. Her favourite song at the time had been, *Baby Come Back* performed by Eddy Grant's band *The Equals,* and she'd never tired of feeding coins into the jukebox to hear it. The boy's grandmother along with her daughter, had fallen for the charms of the man with the Chevy - his flamboyance complimenting her own. Grandad, in contrast to his outgoing wife, had never travelled further than the nearest English seaside resort and hadn't flown or even boarded an aircraft during his entire life. The boy's mother's upbringing had been that of an only child, and life with her father had been a strict affair. He had believed in the maxim that "Children should be seen and not heard" He had kept a cane close by during meal times, and should his daughter forget his rules and dare to reach across to pick up the salt or some other condiment, he'd reward her with a rap across the knuckles with his cane. Family conversations in later years would reveal that as a young married couple, grandma had come home unexpectedly to find her husband in bed with another woman. From that day on, they'd lived separate lives under the same roof. This had even extended to the after dinner routine, whereupon they'd been in the habit of washing their dishes separately!

Grandad hadn't been outwardly unkind to the boys during their stay at number 54 and Ginger particularly liked the game, which had involved his grandfather hiding behind the living room door and jumping out at him shouting "Uff! Uff! Ufff!" (Whatever that meant!) before chasing him through the house. He'd loved Saturday afternoons when they'd all sit down to watch *World Of Sport* on the TV. The highlight of the show as far as the boys were concerned, happened at four-thirty when the wrestling would come on. It had all seemed real to him and he'd been fascinated by the weird and wonderful showmen throwing each other around the ring watched over by the stern faced referees in their black and white striped uniforms. It was the whole goodies and baddies thing again and after the bouts were over and the football scores came on, the boys would be rolling around their grandparent's living room floor pinning one another down and counting like the refs did: "ONE -ER, TWO - ER, THREE –ER... or putting on made up holds before urging each other to submit. Behind the scenes however, plans were afoot for the boy and his family to move into a rented house further down the Avenue at number 5. It had been a bitterly cold November when the family moved into their new home with the only available warmth being in the form of a paraffin *Aladdin* heater around which the family would huddle. It had a safety feature, which meant that if moved or nudged while alight, a guard would slam down and snuff out the flame – not ideal when surrounded by boisterous boys jostling for heat space! Invariably, at some point, the heater would be nudged and have to be relit. The boy's mother also kept an oil lamp burning by the living room window. The lamp was lit every evening and allowed to burn throughout the night and it wasn't until a few months of doing this, that she'd told the boy why. She kept it lit, she'd said, for the man with the Chevy who, it seemed was due to visit any day…

Having not been much more than a toddler when they'd moved to Malta, the boy was suddenly thrust into a strange world of snow, older boys wheeling effigies of Guy Fawkes through his street shouting "Penny for the guy!" and most striking of all; turbaned Indians and Afro Caribbean people. The West Midlands back then had been a booming place of industry, and accordingly attracted workers from far and wide, but the boy would never forget his first ever encounter with a black man. Eyes wide as saucers, he'd innocently remarked – rather too loudly to his brother: "He looks just like a monkey!" The encounter became all the more memorable, when the indignant man strode over to the ginger kid and pushed him into a hedge! He also met older kids who'd showed him how to hide fireworks in their shoes and others who tried to recruit him into their gang of thieves. Their racket involved scaling church roofs to steal the lead, but naive as the boy was in his new surroundings, he'd declined their offer either through fear of getting caught or because he knew it was wrong. It hadn't been long before he'd lost both the fear and his sense of what was wrong though, because a few weeks later, he'd completed his rite of passage by stealing - of all things, some life size plastic house flies from *Woolworths!* Once home, for a laugh, he'd slipped one of the "flies" into his mother's tea. After gamely feigning shock, his mother had asked him where he'd got the plastic insects. He may have overcome the fear of stealing, but he hadn't been equipped with the nous to make up a convincing story, and so within minutes, he'd been escorted by the ear straight back to *Woolworths* to face the manager!

On the day it snowed, the boys built their first ever snowman in the garden of number 5. Ginger's un-gloved hands, freezing and raw, had ran inside to get his mother to come out to admire his handiwork, and there in the sitting room was the man with the Chevy, all bonhomie and bearing gifts. Mum positively beamed and looked happier than he had seen her since they'd left Malta. That evening they'd trooped round to number 54 for dinner. Grandad, introduced to his daughter's lover for the first time, had appeared less than impressed and only forced a tight smile when presented with a bottle of Maltese wine. Later, at the dinner table, when the bottle had been uncorked, grandad had taken a sip before announcing loudly that it: "tasted like bloody cardboard!" From that day on, the old man - ever the diplomat, had referred to his daughter's lover as: "That greasy man" Needless to say, his long-suffering wife, had been her usual impressed self when in the company of the Maltese man, and she'd enthused over his general presence and his gifts to her of duty-free *John Player Specials.*

Unbeknown to the boy, the surprise reappearance of his mother's lover, had not only been planned, but marked the completion of the early stages of his parent's divorce, and so a couple of weeks after the man's arrival, the family locked the door to number 5 Lawfred Avenue for the last time and headed to the airport from where they would fly back to Malta. Also unknown to the boy, was the fact that having left the Islands as the children of a military family at the end of his father's official three year posting, they were now civilians with no rights to settle in the country. Their return also coincided with the winding down of the military garrison and the slow but sure transition to the left-leaning politics of the current government. Accordingly, the British were beginning to lose the welcome extended to them when entreated in 1800 by the islanders to rid their country of the scourge of Napoleon Bonaparte. It wasn't that the islands didn't have anglophiles among the population, but traditionally it had been a fifty-fifty split between those loyal to the Labour Party and the Nationalist Party. In 1971, Mintoff, the leader of the Labour Party, managed to win the election by 4000 votes and soon after, the gradual removal of all British troops from the island had begun. All in all, these hadn't been ideal conditions under which a British family could return to Malta on anything more than a tourist visa. The man with the Chevy and his contacts within the Labour Party had either pulled some strings, or else they had sneaked in under the creaking and antiquated radar.

The boy's new Maltese home was to be 41, Valletta Road in Paola – or as the locals called it Rahal gdid (the new village) Paola bordered Fgura – home to Raymond flats, where the family had lived when with their father. The new house was rented from a landlady so large - that she was barely able to walk - for the princely sum of ten pounds a month. Generally, the boy had been tasked to drop off the rent money and get the rent book signed accordingly. Actually, he had quite enjoyed going to see the landlady and she usually sat him in her darkened parlour with a glass of Vermouth while she shuffled off to her office to sign the rent book. Upon leaving, she would ruffle his tousled red hair before presenting him with a bar of chocolate and sometimes a few coins. Consisting of three floors, the new house was more than adequate for the family's needs with the flat roof space providing not only an adventure playground for the boys, but also the opportunity to roof hop across the adjoining house roofs. Climbing yet higher, onto what the boys called "the top bit" the brothers found that they could shin up the ten-foot poles holding the TV aerials until they were as high as they could go. From the roof, the boys also enjoyed a grandstand view of the daily comings and goings from RAF Luqa, which, still in the hands of the British, launched regular training sorties of Canberra bombers, English Electric Lightnings and that cold war colossus, the Vulcan. As the crow flew, Luqa was only two or three miles, on a direct flight path over the boy's house, and the jets would scream overhead on their final approach to the airfield. It sometimes seemed to the boy that the windows of the house would surely shatter, so low did the planes fly over. One such day on the roof, the boy actually witnessed a Vulcan explode in mid-air, scattering wreckage across the village of Zabbar and doing little to convince the locals that the British should be allowed to stay.

Life had been relatively carefree in the early days of their return to the island and the man had provided for them; delivering crates of fizzy drinks, boxes of fancy cream-cakes and other treats. He used to give the boy a shilling for washing the gigantic Impala muscle car, and climbing up onto the bonnet, he'd sluice it down with countless buckets of water until the old lady across the road had screamed in Maltese, a warning, which roughly translated, meant that he would "Fuck up the engine!" As the financial and emotional strain of keeping two families began to take its toll on the man from Hamrun, life for the English boys became more difficult. The reality was, that the once successful businessman who'd captivated the wife of the airman, had begun to run out of money and business success. The affair had become common knowledge among his official family, and his sisters were rocking the boat. An unsuccessful bid to run as local Labour Party MP followed and the boys, now seen as an unwanted appendage to his English lover, were made to feel more and more unwelcome. The presents dried up, as did the fun days out to the beach and the fun kite flying days up on the sun-baked roof. The man was insanely jealous of anyone – children included - who may have rivalled him in his affections for the woman he'd wooed back in the heady days of the Lucky Bar.

The daily routine at number 41, would involve the man coming home at the end of his day at the TV shop (sometimes he'd appear in the afternoon as if to catch the his woman in some imaginary clinch) He'd lock himself away in the front room with the boy's mother and there he would stay, drinking heavily and chain-smoking cheap local cigarettes. He'd long since given up the fashionable *Du Maurier* in the flash red packets - that he'd smoked back in the successful days before those bastard kids (his words) had bled him dry. He began to beat the boys for the slightest misdemeanour and exerted total control. Even a chance funny remark by the boy's mother about how one of her jobs when a member of the Women's Royal Air Force had been to empty and clean the urine tubes used in flight by fighter pilots, had drawn a completely irrational jealous outburst – how dare she even think about such genitally-related topics! On another occasion, an eccentric English guy who was staying in their road for a few months had visited 41 to explain that he owned a drum kit, and wanted to make sure he wasn't disturbing his neighbours when he practised. (For obvious reasons, the kids had christened the guy - who was a bit of a loon - with the nickname of "drum banger") They'd once witnessed him washing his car. Filling the trunk with the hosepipe, he'd decided that in order to drain away the water, he would drill a hole in the floor of the trunk to drain it out!

When the man found out that the boy's mum had spoken to another man, no matter how innocently, he'd flown into a rage, leaving her sobbing in her bedroom. The sound of his mother sobbing was to become a regular feature to the boy and it had always upset him. With money being scarce, one of the first things to be reluctantly let go was the man's prized Chevrolet Impala. For a while, he borrowed his sister's Ford Escort, but in time bought a clapped out Triumph Herald (ironically the same model and colour as the boy's father had owned when they had lived at Raymond Flats) This one though, had leaked exhaust fumes into the interior and could only be safely driven with the windows open. As for the boy's mode of transport – the scooters they'd brought over from Cardiff – they disappeared one day; the reason for their disappearance, their mum told them, was that she'd "given them away to some poor children" The kids hadn't been impressed, not realising that the scooters had most likely been sold to buy food. The man's business starting to fail: he'd resorted to ripping off his clients, and when a TV would be brought in for what he discovered was a minor repair, he'd clean a couple of valves, or a transformer using methylated spirit and a paintbrush; thus duping the customer into thinking more expensive parts had been replaced. It hadn't been long before the boy's father's monthly £17 alimony cheque was practically the only income coming into number 41.

The boys slowly but surely began to outgrow their clothes and wear out their shoes. They were well beyond each other's hand-me-downs, and when their Mum obtained some clothing from a local charitable source, they had fortunately been too young and oblivious to fashion, to notice that some of the donated clothing had blatantly been pre-owned by females. The boy became the proud owner of a pair of trousers with the zipper fastening at the side, a pair of blue gym shorts with an elasticated waist, and a pair of girls' canvas deck shoes (also elasticated). He'd immediately christened these his *Doris* shoes. His new footwear – girls' or not – seemed to endow upon the boy, the ability to run faster than he had ever run before and despite their feminine appearance, the shoes had put wings on his feet and he sprinted wherever he went. The locals had taken to calling him *Billy Whizz* after the comic book character of the time, but generally, along with his brothers, he'd been known as *L-Ingliz* – The English Boy. A further and more bizarre addition to Ginger's wardrobe had been a pair of oversized Wellington boots – ideal for muddy English fields, but hardly suited to trudging the hot and dusty streets of Malta! Even underwear became a luxury with the lack of socks proving to be a particularly unpleasant experience inside his "Wellies" Once he'd worn his Doris shoes out; his only choice had been the stubbornly indestructible Wellington boots. When it had become unbearingly hot, and the pools of sweat within began to rot his feet, he'd simply gone without, walking miles in his bare feet and leaving them with gaping sore cracks and infected with athletes foot. Coming home with filthy feet, his mum would make him put his feet into the bath to get them clean. Pouring a measure of the local washing powder called *Skip* into the water, she'd amuse herself by saying 'There's Skip in it – so – *skip* in it!' The harsh and corrosive nature of the cheap washing powder had made for a miserable experience for the boy, with the chemicals seeping into his cracked feet and stinging like hell.

Birthdays and Christmas became non-events and presents a thing of the past. One year, as a Christmas present, the Boy In Wellington Boots had been presented with a repaired Big Jim. The boy had long since outgrown his old bear and it had lain forgotten under a bed, its arms practically hanging off, and generally in a sad old state. Big Jim had become a bit of a Cyclops along the trail of neglect and had lost an eye; he hadn't been hugged for a good few years and truth be known, had been only fit for the dustbin. Despite his dilapidation, the boy's mother, short of anything else to give her son for Christmas, had lovingly and skilfully repaired old Jim. Her son had long since grown out of cuddling stuffed toys, but the BIWB had been touched by his mother's gesture and despite his age and growing street wisdom, Ginger had grown to love Big Jim all over again. The only gift he'd been given after Big Jim, had been a couple of years later on his birthday, when as a pressed churchgoer, he'd been given of all things, a rosary; and he'd been expected to be both excited and grateful! He'd tried to hide his disappointment, but it must have been apparent that a string of beads with a crucifix attached to the end, just wasn't cutting it and simply hadn't featured on the birthday wish list of a deprived teenager…

During these hard days, even the basics of life, such as cups to drink from, had become scarce and with each breakage unable to be replaced, the boy's mother had come up with the canny idea of using old jam jars from which her family would now drink their tea! With the blissful ignorance and optimism of youth, most of these things could be endured. What couldn't however, was the man's oppressive and seemingly constant presence, his irrational jealousy and general insecurity. The latter soon manifested itself in his forbidding of the boy's mother to set foot outside the house for fear of another taking her from him, and with this edict; darkness, hunger and misery began to descend over 41 Valletta Road and its occupants…

Part Two

Chapter Three
Punishment And Occasional Nourishment
'The dictionary definition of "bastard" is to have been born out of wedlock – my mum and dad were married...'

Breakfast had become virtually non-existent for the boys; the man would generally arrive at around five am – they never knew why he'd turn up so early unless it had been to check on their mother's fidelity - and turf them out of bed before sending them up to the roof to clean out the rabbit cages. Other household chores would follow and the kids would have to endure the aroma of hot buttered toast knowing that as was usual, the food would be destined solely for the stomachs of the adults. They'd be lucky to be sent to school with a cup of tea in their bellies, although fortunately for the English boys, Maltese schools at that time, dished out not only vitamin tablets to their pupils, but also a half-pint of milk in chocolate, strawberry or vanilla flavours. Sometimes other kids shared their sandwiches with the BIWB and so one way or another, he'd managed to get through the day. Evening meal times at number 41, generally consisted of the man cooking the food (for him and the boy's mother) while the kids sat on the stone stairs outside the firmly closed dining room door. The timing of the man's cooking would normally   be around nine pm, by which time the boys were very hungry indeed. So hungry had they been, that it hadn't been uncommon for them to eat the grain stored up on the roof that was intended for the chickens and pigeons. The boy in wellington boots had even resorted to trying Candy's dog food – not too bad, if a little gritty. During the day, when not at school, he had been known to eat food found on the street; the odd half bag of discarded and cold chips had warded off the pangs of hunger on more than one occasion. He and his brother had sometimes run errands for the guys who worked at the local petrol station and so been able to feed themselves with the local *pastizzi*; cheap but delicious filou pastry parcels containing either ricotta cheese or mashed up peas. Also known as either cheesecakes or pea cakes, they could be bought for pennies, hot from a roadside kiosk. A bit of petty thieving from the grocery

34

store had also become a practical necessity with which to supplement their meagre diet. Standing at the counter, they'd sneakily crumble bits of soft sand coloured nougat from the sickly sweet cake crammed with almonds and known as *Helwa tat-Tork* - sweet of the Turks" Introduced when Malta had been under Arab rule, it was sold by weight and could be found in most grocery stores; Vladi (the shopkeeper) always kept his *helwa* on the counter and sympathetically turned a blind eye to the boy's thieving.

Vladimir Pisani, host to the drum banger, ran the grocery store on the corner of the boy's street; a larger than life character, he was fashionable and trendy, wearing bell-bottomed jeans and the long 70's sideburns of the day. At breakneck speeds, roaring around the neighbourhood with tyres screeching, he'd driven his Ford Cortina Mark One - specially commissioned, liveried and powered by Lotus. His faithful companion had been a jet black Alsatian dog named Prince, whose ears he'd taped to stand up and make him look wolf-like and fiercer! Vladi had loved to shock the older ladies who came into his shop and once, the boy had seen him searching among the vegetable display, before triumphantly producing and holding aloft a long and gnarled carrot, which he'd showed to the women, loudly exclaiming: 'Tal-Papa!' The Catholic ladies had tut- tutted in mock horror at the shopkeeper's irreverent allusion to the Holy Father's genitalia! Vladi's store; typical of the village shops originally built as terrace houses, had every nook and cranny stuffed with produce. The high ceiling allowed for racks of floor to ceiling shelving, but not owning a ladder – and in order to reach those products stored on the uppermost shelves, he'd converted a broom handle with a nail hammered into the end and then bent over to fashion a hook. Using the hook to catch onto the lip of some tin or other, he'd yank it down before deftly catching it; scattering those of his customers foolish enough to have been standing below the spinning and seemingly out of control can! Another method he'd sometimes employ to reach high placed produce, had been that of grabbing the nearest unsuspecting kid by the ankles and hoisting him aloft with the instructions to grab whatever he was after! When not using the boys as human tin grabs, Vladi would fool around with them, and one day when the BIWB; dressed in his usual wellies and shorts, had come into his shop on some errand or another, he'd pulled back the boy's elasticated waistband with the intention of letting it twang back into place. Unfortunately, and unbeknown to Vladi, the BIWB was by now, without underwear – commando so to speak - and patting the red faced boy on the back, Vladi had covered his own embarrassment with a coarse joke. Apart from his blind eye to the boy's helwa thefts, Vladi had from time to time, fed *L-Ingliz* with either sandwiches or doughnuts left over from the day before, and had generally shown him the human compassion he'd lacked at home. The kindly shopkeeper had even implored the man to allow him to adopt one of the kids from number 41; but not wanting to relinquish control, the man had dismissed his humane appeal outright.

Vladi hadn't been the only person to show the kids kindness: across the road from number 41 lived a lovely lady known to the boys - for obvious reasons - as "The Ginger Lady" Antonia lived in a big old house on the corner of Valletta Road with her own kids and a couple of yappy Chihuahua dogs whose party trick had been to smoke cigarettes! In contrast to that of her English neighbours, her house had rung with the sound of laughter and her family had always appeared laid back and living life to the full. Antonia could mostly be found sitting in the sun outside her house and whenever they'd passed her front door, she'd often given the boys a much-needed cuddle and a glass of juice or a bite to eat. Other sources of food and warmth had been provided, along with others, by one of the BIWB's school friends' mother. Raymond had lived a couple of hundred yards up the hill from 41, and when he'd met him to walk up to school together, Ray's mum would sit the ginger kid on her knee, rocking him like a baby. As he sat there, his Wellington booted feet swinging, the lady would lament the fact that like Vladi, she would have loved to have been able to adopt him if only she'd have been allowed.

Another eating opportunity had afforded itself when the boy had been sent to the bakery to buy a loaf of bread. Fresh from the oven, it had been so hot the first time he'd been sent, that it melted its way through the plastic carrier bag he'd taken to carry it back in! Rustic Maltese bread tends to have a panel on each crusty side, exposing the soft layers of white dough within. This, the boy soon learned, could be carefully peeled away leaving identical layers to the original outer and so provide him a sneaky and undetected intake of food for the way home. The boys had become adept at daytime food scrounging, but it was the evenings when their hunger was the most keenly felt. There on the stairs, the brothers had hatched a plan; it involved a chorus of "Can we eat please?" which was to be aimed at the dining room and those within, in the vain hope that this would draw attention to their hunger. Of course, Ginger usually fell foul of his older brother's tricks and when it had been agreed that after a count of three, they would begin the pleading chorus; the older boy would start off with a "Can..." before tailing off and letting Ginger shout the rest on his own! After perhaps an hour or more of calling out to the uncaring adults behind the closed dining room door, the boys would be admitted to find only leftovers. What was more, they wouldn't be allowed to eat the remaining food until they'd washed up the utensils used to make it in the first place. If the dining room was out of bounds, then television was as good as forbidden and the only way the boys would get to view it, had been in the reflection of the kitchen window as they worked their way through the pile of greasy pots and pans. A particular favourite "watch in the window" programme had been David Carradine's *Kung Fu*. The show had been the man's favourite too and so engrossed in it had he been, that he wouldn't notice the boys washing the dishes as slowly as they possibly could in order that they "see" as much of the show as possible! Sometimes, when on the odd occasion the man had left to return to his real family at a reasonable hour, the boy in wellington boots would sneak into the sitting room and convince his mother that as she loved musical films, she should put one on and let him watch it with her. It wasn't as though *he'd* liked musicals, but this had been his chance to seize a rare and precious opportunity to spend some time with his mum.

One summer, the boy's grandmother had arrived and as with her earlier visits to the island during the happier days of "Baby come back" she'd duly appeared at the airport dressed in her usual faux fur and costume jewellery. From the boy's perspective, it seemed that while she was visiting, his mother and the man did what they could to present an atmosphere of normality. The kids got fed and they went on family trips just as they had before. The BIWB however, had been determined to in some way, let his grandmother know just how dire things really were. He'd walk past her with his meagre plate of food and upon reaching her, would theatrically slow down so that she could see how little food he had to eat. Unfortunately for him, his grandma hadn't noticed his subtle and silent plea for help and had merely carried on chatting and chain-smoking her *John Player Specials*. Upon being sent out to buy something or another, Ginger, emboldened by the presence of his gran, actually kept the change from the purchase, spending the money on a doughnut from Vladi's shop. He had reasoned that as long as his grandma was in the house, the man wouldn't dare to punish him and sure enough, he'd been right. When he'd returned from the shops minus the change, he quickly admitted having spent the money on what he pathetically – and to make a point – described as a *stale* doughnut. He had figured that not only would he avoid punishment on this occasion, but he'd also be fulfilling his intention of alerting his gran to the fact that, so hungry had he been, he'd resorted to stealing money in order to buy a doughnut - which hadn't even been fresh! In the event, Ginger had been right about the man not making much of a fuss and he'd avoided physical punishment; but been woefully unsuccessful in his attempts at demonstrating his lack of sustenance to his gran! Charmed by the man who used to drive the Chevy - just like her daughter before her - the old girl had simply departed the island after her holiday thinking all was well with her daughter's family and left the boys to revert to their normal and miserable hungry lives.

There had been times before the real days of hunger, when the boy's mum had done her best to feed her kids. She'd bought pig's heads and trotters from the man from the slaughterhouse who'd made his weekly rounds on his donkey drawn cart; and been inventive with the production of a bewildering array of pate and brawn. Pig's trotters actually hadn't been that bad, it was just the butter beans; soaked overnight and swimming in the gelatinous mess, that had put Ginger off his food. His mum had also made a gallant attempt at recreating baked beans in tomato sauce – a much-loved staple back in their own country. The same beans would be soaked overnight before being tipped into a watery mush of tinned tomato puree, the results would have made Mr Heinz turn in his grave! Of course, a year or so down the line, such culinary disasters would have seemed like a feast! From time to time, the BIWB would be dispatched to the local market where the sprawling stalls with their braying vendors, offered livestock in the form of rabbits and chickens - choose one and witness its unfortunate demise while you wait - and even snails, very much alive and crawling all over the stall. It hadn't been for meat that the boy was sent though, this had cost too much; it was generally for a bunch of what the locals called *Tal-Minestra* – an optimistic take on the ingredients for minestrone soup – and consisting of a wedge of bright orange pumpkin, a couple of carrots, a sheaf of flat leaved parsley and some celery stalks. The first time that the BIWB had been sent to the market to procure the vegetables, a kindly and incredibly wizened old man had taken one look at the skinny ginger boy in the shorts and wellies, and handing him the bunch, he'd waved his weather beaten hands and called out: 'No pay, bye-bye!'

Ginger quite enjoyed his trips to the market for a couple of reasons; one had been, that his walk up the hill had taken him past a car repair shop, the owner of which kept a fully grown orang-utan. The unfortunate creature had probably been bought from a sailor passing through the Grand Harbour and although its owner didn't appear cruel, he nonetheless kept the beast, chained to the garage wall. The boy would always stop and stare in wonder at the primate; which surrounded by oily car parts and tools, looked thoroughly miserable. In its unnatural environment, thousands of miles away from its home in Borneo or Sumatra the orang-utan had spent the day picking and scratching at its ginger fur while gazing miserably out into the street. The garage owner had given it a couple of old tyres with which to play, but this had been no compensation for the lack of forest where its brothers and sisters roamed free. Perhaps the boy had felt he'd had something in common with the chained animal – they'd even shared the same hair colour!

Another place the BIWB loved to linger had been the cobbler's shop in Paola's main square. Despite the pokey interior, the shoemaker had filled all available wall space with aquariums, all teeming with exotic tropical fish. The cobbler hadn't exactly been effusive and seemed to prefer his own company, surrounded by the smell of glue and the bubbling hiss from his fish tanks. This hadn't prevented the boy from trying to get him to chat about the fish though, asking inane questions about what they cost – as though he could afford any of them! If he were lucky, his persistence would occasionally be rewarded with a surly grunt just to get rid of the English kid in the wellies!

Back at home, his mum had on occasion, attempted to cook snails. The boy had been fascinated when upon salt being poured onto the snails in the saucepan; they'd omitted a squealing noise akin to crying. He hadn't realised that this had something to do with the boiling water forcing air into the unfortunate creature's shells and he'd always felt sorry for them. He'd felt even sorrier when he'd tried to eat them later – it had been like eating chewing gum laced with garlic - mum strikes again! Her efforts at cooking octopus hadn't been much better – the obligatory butter beans, tomato puree and a rubbery mess of suckers! Of course this had been before the food had all but run out; the days before lack of staples such as sugar had resulted in his mother using orange flavoured boiled sweets with which to sweeten tea. When sugar had still been available, he'd made use of the sparse foodstuffs in the cupboard and made himself crunchy margarine and sugar sandwiches.

Another more bizarre item to have been eaten by the BIWB had been force fed to him by the man; possessed as he'd been, by a fit of irrational jealousy. Knowing how much his mum loved flowers, the boy had picked a bloom from a neighbour's garden and brought it home for her. The man had felt so threatened by this show of affection towards his woman – albeit from her own son - that he had made the boy eat the flower right there and then in front of his mother. It hadn't been the first time that the man had made the BIWB eat something odd either. When he'd caught him experimenting with cigarettes, he'd again stood him in front of his mother and forced him to eat one. The irony that he himself hypocritically smoked two packs a day - which he'd send the boy out to buy- appeared to have been wasted on him. Actually, by this time, the boy was well and truly on his way to nicotine addiction which he satisfied either from the man's dog ends; which when pinched off from the filters, made enough to fill a pipe he'd found, or by picking up still lit cigarette ends thrown from passing cars. His brother, ever the more cunning of the two, had taught him how to wedge bits of plastic into matchboxes to prevent the contents rattling in their pockets when they walked around the house! He'd also shown him how to make homemade fireworks. This had involved wrapping a piece of striker peeled from a matchbox, around several matches, before further wrapping them in silver foil. The resulting mini-explosion when struck with a hammer had been most satisfying, and had been up there with burning ants to death using a magnifying glass and the scorching August sun up on the roof! The kids may have been hungry and had to endure being beaten, but this hadn't diminished their natural male enthusiasm for all things adolescent, and the discovery of things which could be made to explode, smashed up and generally destroyed! There had also been a couple of juvenile - well meaning - but ill thought out incidents; in which animals had played an unwitting part. A case in point had been the avian Steve McQueen of the budgie world, whose escape attempt had been on par with that of the actor's. The boy's mother hadn't been immune to the 1960's British love affair with budgerigars, and with the man's permission; she'd converted an area of the second bedroom into an aviary. The area had been a kind of annex with a large window, which looked out over the back of the neighbour's back yard, and by partitioning the majority of the space using chicken wire, she'd built up a collection of noisy birds. One eventful day, the BIWB was in the aviary with his older brother, who had decided that the captive birds deserved to taste some freedom. Choosing his victim and uttering the immortal words: "He wants to fly" he'd tied a generous length of string to the poor creature's leg, before letting it fly out of the window. The bird, no doubt, unable to believe its own luck, flew as fast and as far as it could until it cruelly and literally reached the end of its tether! Not wanting to risk the wrath of his mother, he'd proceeded to haul the squawking and bewildered budgie back into captivity, shedding bright green feathers as it was dragged reluctantly back to reality and another case of: "If you tell on me…!"

The flower eating incident hadn't put the boy off picking flowers for his mother, and several weeks later, he'd come across one of the ubiquitous Mediterranean Oleander bushes that grew almost all year round on the island. In contrast to the privately owned flower that he'd been made to eat, he'd found these particular blooms growing on a patch of waste ground. The pink flowers grew in clusters and were quite tough to separate from their stems. The Oleander bush had been growing alongside a spiky palm, the branches of which had become entwined with those of its neighbour. Oblivious to the hidden spikes, the BIWB had tugged a stem downwards in an effort to dislodge it from the unyielding bush. He'd put so much effort into pulling the flowers free, that when the stem finally gave way, his hand had continued forcefully down towards the hidden palm fronds, where he'd encountered a large spike. This had pierced the skin, before painfully entering his wrist and breaking off under the skin and immediately paralysing his lower arm. Along with the pain, it had felt as though something was physically preventing his wrist from moving on any plane. Clutching his fought-for prize of bright pink flowers in his good hand, the boy had taken them home safe in the knowledge that the man hadn't been there. Presenting the wild bouquet to his mother, he'd told her about the spike in his wrist and subsequent paralysis, and they'd both assumed that it had been a temporary condition. Unfortunately, the feeling hadn't returned to his arm for around six weeks, during which time he'd been unable to even write at school. He'd been given no medical attention and had resorted to the only ginger-haired and stubborn solution available – that of self-help. If the damn thing wouldn't bend of its own accord, then naturally or not, he'd make it happen! When it had been time for bed, he'd simply forced the paralysed wrist towards his inner arm, and remaining in this position; he'd slept with his body weight on top of the recalcitrant limb, in an attempt to return it to some kind of normality. Either this unorthodox method or the passage of time, had eventually freed his wrist and another chapter in the boy's history of self-help had been written…

Around eighteen months into his relationship with the English woman, the bankrupt man who used to own the Chevy and now drove the clapped out Triumph Herald, began to show his true colours towards her children. His kindly but pseudo mask had well and truly slipped and his ill-disguised hatred for what had become unwanted baggage started to bubble to the surface. He'd taken to calling them by nicknames, which he'd made up and considered funny. The older boy was named "Scissors" because of his long legs - their skinny and bony shape due in part to malnourishment. He dubbed BIWB as "Pig" because in the man's eyes he was greedy – (chance would have been a fine thing!) The name he gave to the youngest boy was that of "Mouse" possibly because he was the youngest and quietest, but also because he'd been small and made a small squeaking sound when he cried – which was often. The hatred hadn't only manifested itself in the deprivation of food that had crept in to their lives either. He'd also begun to devise some wacky punishments for so-called demeanours; common in childhood, but totally un-tolerated by him. It wouldn't have been an exaggeration to say, that his efforts had bordered on torture. When the BIWB had come home from school one day having learned a new playground song, he'd been keen to sing it to his brother. Mintoff and his Labour party were a couple of years into power and one of the kids at school - whose family had been part of the 50% who hadn't voted for them - had picked up a political song at home which had a chorus of "*Ghaliex Mintoff Communist*…" Translated, this basically accused the prime minister of being a communist and with the Labour government openly courting Libya and China, the words in the song had struck a chord with a lot of Nationalist voters. Unfortunately for the BIWB, the man had been such a staunch Labour supporter, that he had taken umbrage to the English kid's rendition of the playground song. He'd launched into a spittle-flecked rant about how, if it hadn't been for Mintoff and the man's contacts within the party, the family wouldn't have been allowed to remain on the island. By now, it could have been said that in the eyes of the boy, this didn't add up to being a favour! Rant over, the man's favourite punishment had been wreaked on the hapless boy; this basically involved a long cold shower, followed by his being sent - still naked onto the roof, where he would be left to shiver in the night air until such time as the man saw fit to call him back down. Up there on the roof, where even the rabbits and chickens had had shelter, the boy had disobeyed the man's instructions that he keep still, and had roamed around the roof shivering and trying to keep out of the cold wind. He'd kept the anti-Mintoff tune going from between his chattering teeth, in defiance of the bastard below.

Other spurious reasons to mete out punishment had included accusing the boys of mislaying his tools; all denials were dismissed with the bewildering and often used expression: 'You will never be able to deceive me until you have hair coming out of your bottom!' (Presumably he took pride in the fact that he had luxuriant hair growth in that part of his body which in his mind, made him not only older but wiser!) One day, while examining the contents of a jar in which he kept sultanas, he wrongly came to the conclusion that some were missing and that the boys were to blame. He'd decreed that until one of the boys owned up to taking the sultanas, there would be no food for them at all. This went on for two or three days, by which time, the third and youngest boy gave in, "confessed" and was duly punished. Of course, he hadn't taken the fruit at all, but being younger and less resourceful in the food scrounging department than his older siblings, he'd been unable to stand the hunger any longer, prompting his "confession" It hadn't been the first time that the unfortunate younger boy had been coerced into making "admissions" by his brothers and if he'd been reluctant to "come clean" the older boys sometimes took the easy way out of a whodunit scenario and simply blamed him anyway!

On another ridiculous occasion, the man had made a point about the boys not tidying away what had remained of their dwindling playthings, by theatrically pretending to slip on an errant toy car – it hadn't been an Oscar winning performance either – but punishment had followed nonetheless. Kicks and punches weren't uncommon, and such was the intensity of the attacks, the boy's skin would actually smell of the man's pungent aftershave after he'd received a beating from him. He'd taken to calling the kids "bastards" and when the BIWB had looked up the dictionary definition of a bastard and cheekily reminded the man that he had a father and that he'd been born in wedlock, more aftershave transfer had ensued! One evening, Ginger's older brother had been accused of some minor transgression and a novel punishment had been dreamed up. Rather than initially showing anger, the man had handed the unsuspecting boy a foot long piece of thick pig leather along with a tin of shoe polish and brushes, before sending him up to the roof to polish it. The instructions to the bemused boy were; that once he'd brought the leather to a gloss, he was to call the man and show him his handiwork, and this he'd duly done before handing it over for the bizarre inspection. Once in possession of the shiny strip of hide, the man had held it aloft before chasing the unfortunate boy around the roof raining blows down on him as he did so!

When the older boy, aged fourteen, had found a ten-shilling note, he had had the temerity to excitedly talk about how he would be able to buy himself new footwear to replace his long since worn out shoes. The man, angered by the boy's unwillingness to hand the money over, had called him selfish and cast him from the house telling him that he could use the money to make a living on his own. (Ironically, back in the days when the man had done his upmost to impress the English woman; in a moment of ostentation, he'd actually given the BIWB a ten-shilling note, just because he could!) Fast forward a couple of years and the amount of money he'd so easily given away as a present, had caused the man to issue the edict that Ginger's brother wasn't allowed to return home to eat or shelter until late at night, when he would be permitted to return home to sleep. Association by the other boys with the outcast, or sharing their scarce food with him, had been forbidden. Ten shillings wasn't going to last forever, and so he'd stopped going to school and found a job which had paid two pounds a week. When the first week's wages had been due, the man had cynically allowed him to return home so that he could have a share of the money. By coincidence, some time after this, the

BIWB had also found some money, twenty pounds in fact, and quite a sum back then. The two ten pound notes had been inside a plastic wallet and had been dropped by someone in the area of the bus terminus in Valletta. Being the middle child, he'd learned from his sibling's mistakes and had handed it over to his mum. The money had gone towards buying his school uniform, but at least he hadn't been thrown out of the house!

There hadn't been such a thing as a washing machine in the boy's house and all the laundry – bedding and clothing alike - tended to be thrown into the bath whereupon it would be trampled underfoot by the kids in the style of traditional wine making. Once the clothes had been subjected to the less than tender attentions of the boys, they would be attached to the taps by one end and have the water brutally, but effectively, wrung out by twisting the other end. For the more stubborn stains, there was the *Baby Burco* boiler in which the laundry was literally boiled. The boy's mother had improvised a length of sawn off broom handle with which to stir and push the bubbling clothes down to the bottom of the boiler. Caustic soda and years of use had bleached the ad hoc implement snow white and it had become known colloquially as the "boiler stick" and it had been the boiler stick that was to feature during one evening's bizarre punishment. Ginger and his older brother had been play fighting, and at one point, the older boy had ended up falling across a leather pouffe with Ginger biting his leg. Annoyed at having his evening disturbed, the man had dragged them into the living room, where he'd made them re-enact their fight. Brother number one was told to lie across the pouffe while the BIWB was told to bite the boiler stick (representing his brother's leg) and after he'd done this, he was ordered to keep it in his mouth. They were instructed to keep totally still and maintain this weird frozen-in -time tableau, until the man had got bored. This hadn't been the last time the pouffe had been employed as a twisted mode of punishment either; it was to be used on another day to supposedly teach Ginger a sick lesson. The BIWB had made friends with a couple of other kids from the same school that lived in his street, and they would meet up in the morning and walk to school together. They had got into the habit of taking turns to carry all the school bags, and on the morning that the man had driven past them on their way to school, it had been Ginger's turn to carry the other two kid's bags. Later that evening when the man came to reaffirm his total control over the family, he'd summoned the boy into the sitting room and stood him in the corner before placing the heavy pouffe into the boy's arms. This apparently, had been to simulate carrying his friend's school bags and no amount of explaining how they took it in turns, had made any difference to the man's intended punishment. He'd made him stand there until his arms burned and shook with the effort of holding the thing up, before kicking him back out of the sitting room to join his brothers on the steps from where they'd soon begin their hungry chorus of "can we eat please?"

For reasons that even in later life he'd been unable to explain, the BIWB, had done something spiteful, wicked and totally unprovoked to his younger brother. Having been tasked with boiling a kettle and fetching the contents to the man in the bathroom so he could shave using hot water; he'd inexplicably decided to pour the contents of the kettle over his long-suffering young sibling. Having first boiled the kettle in the kitchen, Ginger had carried it through the house and into a bedroom that led to the budgie aviary and the bathroom. There in the bedroom, he'd come across his brother who'd been kneeling on the floor playing with a toy. As he drew level with him, the BIWB had stopped and poured some of the scalding hot water down the neck of his unsuspecting brother. Yelping with pain, the poor kid had raised the roof with his cries, and chaired by the furious man whose shave had been delayed, an inquisition had begun. In time-honoured tradition, the man had assembled the family and instructed Ginger to re-enact his transgression. By now, the BIWB had come up with an explanation to the effect that he had been carrying the kettle through the bedroom when suddenly, without first having seen him, he'd stumbled into his brother and tripped over his outstretched legs! The man wasn't having any of it, and using Ginger's older brother as an actor in his latest production, the unshaven man had placed him in the position previously held by the young burns victim. The BIWB was then instructed to enter the room – this time with a kettle filled with harmless cold water - and to demonstrate how he'd tripped over his other brother's legs. He'd taken it to the point of making Ginger re-enact the so-called trip, and much to the disgust of his older brother, he'd been made to actually tip cold water down the disgruntled boy's neck! Not satisfied with the first take in his production, the man had compelled Ginger to act out his misdemeanours several times until his brother had been soaked through and the man had grown bored and reluctantly accepted the boy's spurious explanation!

As the boy's brother had grown older, so he'd become bolder and he'd begun to react to the man's beatings in a defensive way. David Carradine and Bruce Lee Kung Fu mania was sweeping the world, and had spawned a whole new industry taken advantage of among others, by the publishers of the "Teach yourself books" range. They'd added a "Teach yourself karate" book that the boys had somehow managed to get hold of. Martial arts had taken the place of their previous love of wrestling, and up on the roof, Ginger's brother had had him tossing ceramic tiles into the air for him to punch and smash in mid-air. Hard on the heels of tile breaking, had come the inevitable attempts at breaking wood with a "karate chop" Mostly, the reality of such endeavours had usually ended with the wood left unbroken and hands and fingers scraped, bruised and bleeding! Upon discovering this possible threat to his dominance, the man's insecurity had extended to the confiscation of the book, and having done so, he'd proceeded to tear out all of those pages perceived to have been helpful to the boys in defending themselves from his punches and kicks! Despite his actions, the boys had hailed this as a bit of a victory: in that by destroying their book, he'd displayed a hitherto unseen weakness, revealing a chink in the bully's armour. The boys hadn't yet been in a position to exploit their new-found chink, but positive thinking one day, had appeared to have borne a most satisfying result…

Ginger's brother; roped into helping the man with some DIY, believed that through the power of his mind, he'd actually brought about injury to his figure of hate. He'd been tasked to hold one end of a piece of wood that the man was sawing. The man, engaging in some carpentry, had been utilising the stone steps - from where the boys sat in hunger each night – as an improvised workbench. As was his habit, the man had been barefoot, and staring at his bare feet - hatred burning in his eyes – his young assistant had willed something nasty to happen to him. The man had carried on sawing lengths of timber until the boy's mother had brought out a cold drink for him; it had been a hot day, but as had been usual, the boy hadn't been offered a drink. He'd watched in disgust as the man took a long swig before setting the glass down on the steps and carrying on with his work. Suddenly, his sawing efforts had somehow knocked the glass over, whereupon it had bounced down the steps and onto the tiled floor, where it had shattered into a hundred pieces. Startled and taken unawares, the man; object of the boy's earlier hateful thinking, dropped the saw and stumbled down the now wet steps in a vain attempt to stop the tumbler hitting the floor. Too late, he remembered the fact that he wore no shoes, and his stumbling steps had pushed him right onto the broken shards of glass. He'd cut his feet to ribbons and in doing so, had brought a stealthy smile of satisfaction to the face of "Scissors" who he'd previously cast out of the house – ironically, for having wanted to buy a pair of shoes of his own – small victories!

Another dreamed up "lesson" had been to force Ginger to go to Vladi's shop past, quite literally, a pack of snarling stray dogs. The BIWB had been petrified of dogs ever since the incident years before in Fgura, when the dog had been set on him and had bitten a chunk out of his inner thigh. Disregarding the boy's fear, the man's twisted logic had been, that by sending him out to face the dogs, the boy would overcome his fear of them! His generosity had even extended to showing Ginger how to scare the dogs away and had consisted of the instruction that he was to pretend to pick up a stone from the street, before making as if to hurl the imaginary stone at them. In practice, this had initially scattered the animals, only for them to quickly regroup and chase the Wellington boot-shod boy all the way to the shop!

On most (mercifully) dog-free evenings, the man, would send the BIWB to scour the shops for his cigarettes of choice: foul smelling, cheap and nasty, the locally made *Caravan* smokes had replaced the comparatively deluxe *Du Maurier* of the man's more affluent days. A shop that may have stocked the brand in limited quantities on one day hadn't necessarily had them the next, and it hadn't been uncommon for the boy to spend hours and walk miles, from village to village in his quest for the crappy cigarettes. Returning home without them not being an option, he'd been compelled to continue searching, sometimes long into the night. He'd enterprisingly put his travels to good use, and along the way, he would sneak around the back of dusty roadside bars and locate the owner's stack of empty bottle crates. Once he'd found them, he'd stealthily remove a couple of empties, before presenting the bar owner with his own bottles and claiming the two cents deposit! In this way, not only could he buy *pastizzi*, but also the odd cigarette (which when purchased separately, conveniently cost two cents) Ironically, the smokes he bought in exchange for the bottles, were of a far superior quality to the rank *Caravan* ones he'd been sent out to buy. Result? - BIWB 1 - The man 0!

Apart from the seemingly endless hunt for *Caravan* cigarettes, the fact that his mother was confined to the house, it had generally been the boy who invariably carried out errands to the shops. It had seemed though, that no matter what he brought back, he'd usually end up returning with the wrong items, only to be faced with the embarrassment and awkwardness of youth when having to go back and face the irritated shop keeper. He'd be sent to the capital to buy valves, resistors, condensers, capacitors and all manner of components required by the man to repair TV's and radios and sometimes he'd get it right, but sometimes he'd return to the man's shop with the wrong item, only to be sent straight back. To be fair to his mother, there had been the odd occasion, where sending Ginger back to the shop, had been justified: like the time, when sent out to buy loose cheese, he'd returned and watched in horror as his mum; upon opening the greaseproof wrapping had been confronted with maggots crawling from the holes in the cheese! Back to the shop he'd been sent; on this rare occasion, feeling more indignant than embarrassed. The grocer, not comprehending what all the fuss was about, had merely shrugged off the boy's protests before cutting a piece from the maggot-free end of the cheese block, wrapping it up and sending him on his way. Once home, the boy hadn't bothered to enlighten his mother on the fact that he'd brought back another piece of cheese from the same maggot infested batch and he'd saved himself being sent straight back!

Chapter Four
School
'A difficult boy...'

Being estranged from his father and by no means officially in the country, the boy could no longer attend his old school Verdala and so it had somehow been arranged that he be enrolled at the local government school in Paola. With the resilience of youth, the BIWB had got on with being yet again the new boy and had made friends who'd began to teach him Maltese; first a few choice swear words, closely followed by numbers. During the hot days of summer when the schools had only opened for half days, it had been all the hungry English kid could do to remain awake and alert, never mind learning his times tables. He'd been more interested in learning how to catch one of the omnipresent flies that buzzed ceaselessly above his head, and by observing the other kids, he'd become adept at stealthily moving his hand ever closer to a fly on his desk before scooping it up into his fist. Once there, he would hurl the creature onto the floor with enough force to stun it before stamping on it. Sometimes, he'd pick up a dazed fly from the floor and pull off its wings, with a sickening popping sound, and then watch it walk around on his desk desperately trying to figure out why it could no longer fly! The Form teacher Mr "V", had dubbed the boys who occupied themselves with tormenting the flies as *Il-kaccatur ta'dubbien* (hunters of flies) Mr "V", a staunch Labourite, was either just naturally a cantankerous old bugger, or else for political reasons, he didn't like the English; either way, he'd made it his aim in life to make the boy's school life a miserable experience. His way of controlling his pupils had involved shoving a stubby, bitten fingernail digit down inside his charge's collar bones, pulling them to their feet by the sideburns, or administering punishment by way of a piece of wood that looked as though it had been part of a chair in a former life. He'd lovingly named the instrument of torture *Cettina*, (pronounced *Chettina*) and he'd wielded it in the manner of a traditional cane back in the boy's native country. One of the other teachers had been so short of stature that he was infamous for standing on a chair and bringing down his stick as he jumped back off - ensuring maximum momentum! There had been a rumour going around the boy's school, that if you could get hold of a strand of horse hair and place it on the hand about to be whacked with *Cettina*, the strength of the hair would shatter the wood. Had the BIWB ever managed to get hold of some horsehair, he might have put the theory to the test, but it had been an experiment that had remained unproven.

At the slightest provocation, and with monotonous regularity, Mr "V" would send Ginger to stand outside the classroom in the hope that the headmaster, while doing his rounds, would spot the unfortunate boy and punish him further. What the teacher didn't know, was that should the headmaster's approach be imminent, the boy would simply leave his post and walk past him with a cheery 'Hello Sir' before going to hide in the washroom until the head had returned to his office! The deputy head, in contrast with Mr "V", had been a bit of an anglophile and had hit upon the idea that by listening to books being read aloud by an English kid would improve the pronunciation of his fellow pupils when learning to read in English. From time to time – much to Mr "V"'s disgust - the boy would be summoned to read aloud into a tape recorder and invariably, the story he'd get him to read had been the *Ladybird* book about the three little pigs. The deputy head had grown increasingly frustrated whenever the boy said the word "pigs" (which unsurprisingly in a story about three little pigs was quite often) The source of the frustration had been the fact that the BIWB tended to whistle the "s" on the plural of "pig" and try as he may, he just couldn't stop it happening. The source of this inability to prevent whistling on the "s's" had come about after an altercation with public transport:

One day, wearing his Doris shoes and sprinting about in his Billy Whizz type way, he'd run straight into a bus while running absentmindedly across a main road. Close to the main square in Paola. The next thing he'd known was waking up in hospital, where enjoying the rare fuss, it was found that apart from a broken front tooth, he had been uninjured. The bus incident was to initiate several visits to the dentist in the island's capital Valletta, where he'd been at the mercy of Maltese version of the National Health Service. Standing in the lobby of the dentist's surgery, the boy had looked up to see a canvas bucket being lowered to the ground floor containing a set of dentures! When it had been his turn to be seen, it was soon discovered that years of neglect had resulted in several rotten molars. Rather than fill them, the dentist had simply yanked them all out! He'd done a repair job on the boy's broken tooth that had involved a kind of metal post screwed into the remnants of the boy's broken tooth, with the idea of placing a cap over it in the future. In the meantime however – much to the deputy head's growing frustration - the gap in his front teeth would cause a whistling sound whenever he tried to pronounce an "S"

The fact that in the eyes of Mr "V", the BIWB was being pulled out of his class for what he perceived to be preferential treatment really hadn't done anything to endear him to his sadistic teacher. One day, after talking to his mum about his difficulties with Mr "V", she'd written a letter for him to take to his teacher. The delivery of the letter had backfired, and rather than go some way to making the boy's life easier, it had simply served as a source of power to Mr "V". He'd actually opened the letter in front of the whole class, and seizing upon one of the sentences within, he'd read aloud the part where his mother had explained that her son was "A difficult boy!" His teacher had loved it; had actually roared with laughter, and whenever the mood took him, he'd sneeringly refer to the hapless ginger kid as a "D" boy! Things became worse when a newly opened private school – Mount Carmel College in Santa Venera – advertised several free scholarships to bright pupils. The boy never did know how or why he'd been chosen to take up the scholarship, but what he did know, was that the news had been greeted with incredulous scorn by Mr "V" who now took every opportunity to mock the English kid. Bringing him regularly to the front of class, he'd get him to attempt impossible arithmetic on the blackboard with a sarcastic: 'Come on Mount Carmel Boy!' The English kid had been relieved to get away from Mr "V", the bullying and his assistant Cettina

The BIWB's new school was eight miles and two bus rides away from his home in Paola. Mount Carmel college was situated in Santa Venera - just past Hamrun, where the man had his TV repair shop. Tacked onto a Carmelite monastery and its church, it had been a forward-looking establishment, run by a charismatic rector, Father Renato Valente. The school uniform of chocolate brown, with the badge of Mount Carmel on the breast pocket of the blazer, was smart and unlike anything he'd worn since the days of Verdala School. A white nylon shirt complete with 1970's floppy collar and tie, completed the ensemble and best of all, he had, for the first time in years, become the proud owner of a pair of proper school shoes. His old faithful Wellington boots had hardly been appropriate footwear for his shiny new uniform! (They would still have to be worn when out of school clothes though, to make his new shoes last) The twenty pounds he'd found at the bus terminus had been sufficient to buy the entire uniform; with money left over with which to purchase the sheets of brown paper required by the school to cover his textbooks.

The boy hadn't exactly been at the college out of merit, and the other pupils; sons of notaries and well off businessmen, had easily outshone him. Despite this however, he'd fitted in fairly well and been more or less accepted by the other kids. There had been exceptions though and being the new boy yet again, he'd at some point got into a fight with one of the other boys in the playground. Swinging wildly at his tormentor, the BIWB had missed the other kid's head with his fist, connecting instead with his forearm. The resulting impact had fractured Ginger's arm; a diagnosis made later when of his own accord, he'd visited Nurse Baker the ex-nurse from his old school Verdala. Nurse Baker had coincidentally decided to spend her retirement on the island and moreover, she'd actually chosen Paola in which to settle. The old girl had examined his arm and said that he'd probably suffered what she called a "greenstick" fracture; that is to say, a fracture in a soft bone in which the bone bends and partially breaks. He'd gone to hospital and had his arm encased in plaster, but after a couple of weeks, the boy had taken it upon himself to cut the plaster cast off using a pair of garden secateurs! On another occasion, when one of the more affluent boys had brought in an expensive toy to show his classmates, Ginger had asked to see it before inexplicably breaking it in two. He hadn't really been able to explain his actions; a child psychologist may have possibly put it down to jealousy and his unloving environment at home or perhaps his austere existence; bereft as it had been of such luxuries as toys.

One day, while his arm had still been in plaster, he'd done something to upset one of the teachers, who'd actually hit out at him in frustration. Upon returning home that day, the boy had told his mother and thought no more about it. The following day, while sitting in the classroom for a lesson given by the teacher who'd lost it with him, he had been daydreaming and paying no interest in the lesson whatsoever, when the door flew open with a crash and in stalked the man! Going straight up to the teacher, the man had punched him before wiping the floor with him. Leaving the unfortunate teacher in an embarrassed heap on the floor, Ginger's mother's lover strode back out of the classroom and school without a word! For a while, the boy had been the talk of Mount Carmel and if he'd been honest, he would have admitted that he had basked in the attention of his peers and notoriety of his unofficial stepfather. It had probably been the only time since the man had entered the boy's life that the man had actually done something positive for him, and he'd never understood why.

Mount Carmel had mainly employed civilian teachers, but also retained several priests, one of whom – for obvious reasons – taught religion. He was an odd character who throughout his interaction with his young pupils, would never seem to actually look the boys in the eye; rather, he'd deliver his lesson in a monotone voice while looking at a spot on the wall somewhere above the boy's heads. Strangely, he would spend the entire period of instruction with his hands stuck deeply inside the front of his pants where he'd continually fiddle around. The boy may have suspected that the priest had been playing with himself, but the shock of the man beating up the priest's colleague and the thought of an encore, had prevented him from ever reporting the holy man's pocket billiards to his mum!

Having red hair on an island inhabited predominantly by black-haired people, the boy had stood out from day one and the rumour at the school had been that he had dyed his hair. One of the teachers decided one day to settle the argument once and for all by taking one of his hairs and examining it under a microscope but needless to say, such a primitive test had proved inconclusive! Unlike his old school under Mr "V", apart from teaching Italian and French – for which Father Valente had a passion - Mount Carmel had encouraged biology and science; regularly setting the pupils practical homework tasks. Among the more bizarre homework tasks, had been the instruction to catch either a frog or a lizard and dissect it - while still alive - at home. The teacher had issued the boys with a scalpel, before explaining that this should be done humanely. In the absence of an anaesthetic, he'd said, the boys were to employ a crude alternative, which entailed pushing a needle between the eyes of the unfortunate creature and waggling it around to - in the words of the teacher – "destroy its brain cells". He had reasoned that in doing so, the cells, which transmitted pain, would also be destroyed! This the boy had faithfully done while sitting on the stairs back at home. Another practical homework assignment had followed the day's lesson on electricity and conductivity. The teacher had explained that acid was a good conductive material and that using a battery, a bulb, some wires and a container of acid, it should be possible, by dipping the wires into the acid, to complete the circuit between battery and bulb and theoretically produce light. When asked by one of the boys where they could obtain acid, the teacher had assured them that urine contained acid and peeing in a container would be a suitable substitute. That night, back on the dimly lit stairs, the BIWB had filled one of his mum's jam jars with pee and dipping the wires to his contraption into his homemade "acid" he'd made the contact with the battery and bulb, only to observe not the remotest flicker of light! The teacher had either been employed beyond his scientific capabilities or else he'd literally been taking the piss out of his gullible pupils!

Whilst on the subject of acid and its properties; the boy, having shown a wart which had developed on his finger to a classmate, had been reliably informed that, as "over the counter" remedies for warts had contained a form of acid to burn away the hardened and dead skin, all he'd need to do was to get hold of some acid and apply it to the wart. Knowing that unlike pee, car batteries definitely did contain acid, he'd opened up the hood to the man's old Triumph Herald and unscrewed one of the caps to the battery. Dipping a matchstick into the corrosive bubbling liquid within, he'd applied the stuff to his wart. By repeating this procedure every day, he had actually managed to get rid of the wart and mighty proud he'd been too! Unlike the mischievous advice of a guy who lived on his street; that to cure his new squeaky school shoes, he should oil them (which he had eagerly done using the man's red oil can to make a right old mess of his shoes) his school friend's acid advice had actually been accurate!

Father Valente, with his modern thinking, had literally been instrumental in giving the BIWB something of a temporary escape from the grim deprivations of 41 Valletta Road. At the time, Jesus Christ Superstar had burst onto the scene and was taking the world of musical stage production by storm. Hitching a ride on the popularity of the show, the rector decided to put together a school choir, the material for which was to be taken from Jesus Christ Superstar. Father Valente had taken his school choir on tour around the island, culminating in a televised open-air concert in a large square, just within the gates of Valletta. It had to be said that the English boy wasn't exactly blessed with a singing voice, but once again, just like when he'd been mysteriously selected for the college, he'd been thrown another lifeline. With the enthusiastic Father Valente at the helm and conducting the newly formed choir, the boys had been put through their paces learning songs from the show. The boy's favourite had been that sung by Mary Magdalene with the opening line of: *"I don't know how to love him – what to do, how to move him..."* Another song, this time from *Cabaret*, had also been learned word for word by Ginger while sitting on the stone steps back at home. The lusty singing of: *"Oh Fatherland, Fatherland, show us a sign..."* was to be the grand finale of their road show and having never seen the play, he'd wondered in later life why they had sung a song; originally a *cappella* performed by a waiter in the original stage show, but which had descended into the Nazi inspired marching song of *"Tomorrow belongs to me"* At the time, his knowledge of such things had been restricted to war comics in which German soldiers had referred to their country as the "Fatherland" and so he'd suspected a German connection and even at such a young age, had mused on why the Rector of a school in a country so ravaged by the Germans during the war, had wanted the boys to sing German patriotic songs! The truth of the matter probably was, that Father Valente, full of hope for the future of his country and his pupils, had most probably adopted the song for the patriotic inspiration of his young pupils.

The BIWB's main avenue of escape from the misery of home life had been to read, and his favourite place to do this had been at the top of the stairs that led to the roof. There, with the light from the roof door spilling into his "library"-cum-reptile experimentation lab, he'd devoured the print from anything he could get his hands on, staying there until the evening light had failed. His favourites had included *Treasure Island* by Robert Louis Stevenson, *Gulliver's Travels* by Jonathan Swift and a tatty but voluminous book titled *Percy Westerman's Omnibus*, which he'd found from goodness knows where. Such classic works as these had enabled the BIWB to escape the depravations of his own life and "travel" to – in the case of Gulliver, to fantastical and mythical places – and with Westerman, to the other side of the world and far off countries the like of which he could only imagine, such as Hong Kong and the USA. This wondrous world had been brought to life in his hideaway; transporting him from the miserable stone steps of reality, to a colourful world of adventure; a world without hunger, punishment and loneliness. Sometimes, if he could get his hands on some hard to come by batteries, he'd continue to read long into the night using an old flashlight. A combination of reading in poor light and a wholly inadequate diet had resulted in regular crops of painful styes on one or both eyes. Without medical attention or suitable medication, he'd gone along with the totally useless remedies suggested to him by the well-meaning old women of the village, such as cold tea bags or rubbing the affected area with a gold ring.

At one point, the boy had got hold of a copy of the *Readers Digest* that he'd taken to school to read in his break. One of the teachers had spotted him reading the magazine and it had been confiscated. No reason had been given for this action, but in retrospect, that particular edition may have contained some form of adult material deemed unsuitable for the innocent catholic boys of Mount Carmel; ironic really when you took into account the priest with his hand down his pants! The boy's stay at Mount Carmel was in the event, to be a brief one, during which he benefitted from the excellent ethos created by Father Valente and the kindness of his staff. Academically, distracted as he'd been by events at home, he'd hardly excelled – that is unless you counted the sticking of needles into the foreheads of unfortunate creatures in the name of science! A relatively short time after his arrival at the college, circumstances would necessitate a timely intervention by the Rector and a very different kind of attendance at the facility to which he'd won a scholarship and escaped the clutches of Mr "V" with his snide remarks and his beloved *Cettina*...

Chapter Five
Bicycles, Buses And Failed Business Ideas
'Do you think you can fool me?'

(Maltese buses played a large part in the English kid's lives even though they'd not had a clue as to the history of the old bangers.)

The closure of the island's only (and very limited) railway service in 1931, brought about a change in what had hitherto been a limited bus service. A regular island wide service was brought in with the buses being liveried in different colours dependent on their routes. Initially, the colours were designed to be more identifiable to those who in those days hadn't been able to read the destination boards. Pet names for the vehicles, such as: *Florida, New York , California, Impala* and *Turandot* - which had been habitually painted on the sides of the buses - were now discouraged by the newly formed *Gasan* Company, with the proviso that they could be retained, if painted in smaller letters on the sides of the bonnets instead. After the war, owner-drivers owned the majority of buses and the vehicles were sourced from what had been left of pre-war buses. These had included: Dodge 3132's Ford V8's, and Fordson Thames ET7's - the chassis of which, were married to bodies assembled locally by several bus bodybuilders. Others were manufactured from the surplus of wartime ex-military vehicles, such as troop carriers, petrol tankers and even ambulances. In the 1950's and 1960's bodybuilders like Zammit, Barbara, Schembri and Sammut, worked miracles with the abundance of left over British and American military vehicles, and with skill and flair, they began to assemble buses that reflected the excitement of the day. After all, these were the days of rockets into space and wildly ostentatious American cars with outrageous fins and lashings of chrome. All the flashy and modern details of a brave new world began to be represented by skilled Maltese craftsmen thousands of miles away from Cape Canaveral in the USA with their space age designs manifesting themselves in the building of buses. The space theme was represented by such decoration as chromium rockets running along old Ford Thames bonnets.

Their imagination unleashed, the bodybuilders began to incorporate flamboyant Cadillac-type tail fins into the designs for the rear of their buses. Unrestricted, and uninhibited in their transformation of the old military vehicles into buses, the sky had been the limit. The end result had been one never seen before anywhere else in the world and the owner-drivers added to the eccentricity of the exterior by cladding the inside with the new fangled *Formica* with which to create panels to mimic wood grain and marble. They customised their cab areas with either religious shrines; complete with flickering candle-effect bulbs, or famous quotations from films or pop songs of the day. The most popular quotation, often writ large on the back of their cabs had been the Latin inscription, in flowery script, bearing the words: *"Verbum Caro Factum Est"* Taken from the first line of the Benedictine Monk's chant, it translated to mean: *"And the word became flesh"* A bell for the passengers to request a stop was usually hung at the front of the bus and was operated by pulling on an ingenious system of washing line rope; strung the length of the bus.

By the time the BIWB and his brothers arrived in Malta, these same buses with their surly but proud drivers, had cheaply transported millions of passengers on their hard seats, throughout the length and breadth of the islands. During the boy's turbulent stay, the only visible change to the buses had been in 1973, when the old colours, apart from three, had been done away with. A couple of years after the BIWB's departure, they'd all adopted the same colour scheme of light green. Despite the small size of the island (17 miles long by 9 wide) the boy generally didn't stray from the green bus route, which ran from the Three Cities to Valletta, via his village of Paola. By jumping on the light green bus outside Vladi's shop, he could reach both the capital to run some errand or other, and the man's shop in Hamrun, where he took it in turns with his brother to work. The only time he'd changed bus routes, had been when he'd started school at Mount Carmel in Santa Venera. Back then, the proud arrogance of the drivers had been matched only by that of their conductors - lofty fellows, who wore their white peaked caps low and leapt off the bus at each stop before it had actually come to a standstill. The conductors had only been outdone in their haughtiness by the occasional ticket inspector, who would board the bus, generally with the peak of his cap "slashed" and pulled out from the manufacturers intended position, to the point that it's wearer's eyes couldn't be seen. They had prided themselves in their appearance, exuding an almost military bearing, as they strutted among the seats. Randomly and wordlessly thrusting out a hand in demand of a ticket, they'd one-handedly, tear it using only a long-nailed thumb to rip through the cheap paper, before handing it back. The boy had learned, that the inspectors rarely checked everyone's tickets, and observing those passengers who more than likely hadn't paid for their fare; he found that, by looking steadfastly out of the window as the inspector passed, he could normally escape detection. That being the case, he would be up on the deal by tuppence with which he could get himself some food! When the inspectors dismounted the bus, it would be at even higher speeds than that of the conductors and with more panache. The kids, impressed with what they saw, used to try to emulate them; jumping, then running backwards, little feet slap-slapping on the tarmac as they tried to compensate for the momentum of the departing bus and the reality of the ground rushing up to meet them. Although this manoeuvre could, in a fashion, be carried out by an English boy in his oversized Wellies, it wasn't to be recommended! The ancient buses would be put to good use by other non-paying passengers too, and Ginger had been quick to learn the trick. While riding a bicycle, the kids would approach a stationary bus at a stop; then making sure they were on the driver's blindside, they would simply grab hold of the huge chrome bumper at the rear with one hand, while keeping hold of the bike handlebars with the other. Hanging on for dear life, they'd get a free if hairy tow from the unsuspecting bus driver. When later the BIWB got to ride his brother's bike, he was to employ a similar trick with near disastrous consequences!

The man had been a frustrated entrepreneur. He'd been awash with ideas and was a skilled enough craftsman to put his ideas into practice – but although his ideas appeared sound, they'd never made business sense and had invariably never got off the drawing board. Later, with the added practical skills and enthusiasm of the boy's mother, some schemes had progressed beyond the drawing board only to fill 41 Valletta Road with half-baked and half- finished products. Back in the heady days of Chevrolet Ramblers, Impalas and the bar with the jukebox that played *Baby Come Back,* the man's television import and repair business had flourished, but with more and more big names arriving from Europe and making obsolete his "sole importer" status, he'd slowly gone under. Reduced to the repair of TVs tape recorders and radios, his shop had begun to resemble a forlorn junkyard piled high with defunct TVs - the majority of which had been well beyond his repairing capabilities. As the mountain of sick television sets grew, he'd had to find ever more ingenious ways of fobbing his customers off. As his interest in the repair business waned, the man; ex-sole importer of Dutch televisions into Malta, increasingly tasked the BIWB and his older brother with minding the shop, taking the flak from frustrated customers, and concocting tall tales of fictional parts on order, out of stock valves and imaginary collection dates. The customers, frustrated as they'd been, were, in most cases either too polite or kind to berate the young boys and had left the shop with no more than a pocketful of promises. None of this had bothered the boys too much; what did upset them, were the sporadic visits by the man's sisters - who storming into the shop, would begin to shout at the boys calling their mother a whore, a shit and many other choice and very un-catholic names!

When the man had graced the shop with his presence, he was generally visited by at least one flunky, who'd hang around the shop for a few hours putting the world to rights and drinking lots of tea. The boy was normally sent to buy the teas from a backstreet bar. There, in the warm fug of local men and their banter, he'd watch as the owner spooned huge quantities of tea into a giant strainer before pouring the contents of a scalding hot kettle over it and into a forest of glasses. Made with sweet condensed milk and served in tall glasses, it would be carried back to the shop inside a cut down Coca Cola crate, which held six glasses, and if he were lucky, he'd be allowed to drink one of them. One particular loathsome visitor to the shop had been a bus conductor; skinny, ugly and spotty, the BIWB had hated him. Seeing the man mistreat the boy, he would seek to ingratiate himself with the boy's tormentor by repeating the man's insults and pretending he was about to hit the boy (this had been another of the man's tricks – that of raising his hand as if he were about to strike the boy – just for a laugh) A frequent and favourite tactic used by the man to belittle the boy, had been to call him "stupid" and picking up on this, the spotty bastard of a bus conductor had found it amusing to repeat the insult over and over again. He enjoyed it so much, that he'd even shortened the word to "Stupe" When in later years, the BIWB thought about the bus conductor from the man's shop - despite the passage of time - he'd known that had he ever met him again, he would have been quite capable of cheerfully kicking him to death!

Besides using the kids as free shop minders, the man had occasionally employed a young guy to provide a more professional service to his customers than that given by the children. This would normally be a kind of apprentice; someone who either had some kind of electrical knowledge, or at the very least an interest in the field. Of these helpers/apprentices, the BIWB had got on well with a couple of them, but not so the pervert - who having just locked up the shop for the day, had called the boy out into the back yard. When Ginger had gone out the back, he'd been faced with the filthy bastard holding his erect cock in his hands, inviting the kid to touch it! Faced with the smiling loser whose pubic thatch looked like an exploded horse hair sofa; the like of which the boy had never seen, he'd fled and gone home to tell his mother. He never did know what had become of the flasher, but he'd never seen him again. There had been the odd happy interlude to be enjoyed in the back yard; such as the day he'd found a fledgling sparrow that had fallen out of it's nest; finding it on the dusty floor of the yard, he'd hand-fed it soggy bread dipped in milk until it had been strong enough to fly away. The BIWB had also hidden cigarettes stolen from the man's packet, among the junk in the yard and he'd defiantly lit them up when he'd been left alone and in charge of the shop. There, puffing away, he'd listen to the sound of the Rediffusion set floating down from the house above. He'd grown up with Rediffusion, and although its broadcasts hadn't particularly interested him, he'd somehow felt it homely and comforting. Perhaps, because it had represented community, he'd latched on to it as a way of belonging.

In 1935, radio broadcasting began in Malta by a company called Rediffusion (Malta) Limited, which had been given the power and authority by the Government to operate sponsored radio programmes as well as ordinary commercial radio programmes. The station: Rediffusion Radio was initially launched, with the aim of countering Fascist propaganda from Italy. It had been given a complete monopoly of the broadcasting of news, features, music and entertainment to about 50,000 subscribers. In February 1960 the Government issued a statement on the future of television and sound broadcasting, saying that Malta should have its own television service as soon as it could be introduced. The Governor of Malta entered into discussions with Rediffusion, with a view to negotiating an agreement with them for the provision of a television service, and the continuation of sound broadcasting in Malta. Rediffusion was to have the sole right of presenting news, views and entertainment to the people of Malta. Television sets were a very expensive luxury to the Maltese, and radio was still the dominant form of entertainment well into the 1970's. In 1975 broadcasting services passed under the control of the State after decades of being a monopoly in the hands of Rediffusion.

One of the boy's more onerous tasks while working at the shop had been that of debt collecting on behalf of the man. These debts had mainly arisen from the TVs he'd sold on credit to the poorer families of Hamrun and presumably, the struggling businessman had reasoned that his debtors would take pity on a scrawny boy in Wellies and pay up their long overdue arrears. And so he'd send him to collect from all manner of down and out folk who'd inhabited the most intimidating of places. The building he had hated being sent to the most, had been ironically, the same apartment block in which the bus conductor of "Stupe" fame lived. The filthy government social housing apartments, with their dimly lit interiors stinking of urine and cheap aniseed alcohol, had been in the same backstreet as the bar from where the boy bought tea.

The apartment block could have only been described as a warren-like hovel, where most of the man's debtors appeared to live. Largely inhabited by stay-at-home alcoholics, the debtors would generally plead poverty, before ushering the boy back out onto the stinking landing and returning to their unpaid for TV and alcohol induced stupefaction.

Someone the boy hadn't minded being sent to see, had been none other than Joe "The Magician" – of the magical coin from behind the ear production fame - who had inhabited the boy's earlier and happier years on the island. Disappointingly, it had seemed that Joe was just a boring old postman who worked at the Hamrun postal sorting office, and hadn't been a magician at all! The reason the man would send the BIWB to see Joe, was so that he could pick up the post for the shop before it was delivered in the traditional way. The boy's illusions about the postie may have been shattered, but he'd looked forward to his visits, and old Joe's wide smile and twinkling eyes had always cheered the lad up.

The storage room at the rear of the shop was crammed with old junk such as irreparable TV sets, miles of jumbled and tangled electrical cable, rusting tools, repair equipment and piles of old 78 records. The floor was literally ankle deep in rubbish and unfortunately for the BIWB and his brother; it had provided more spurious reasons to anger the man. Deciding that he needed some piece of equipment or special kind of tool, he'd send the boys rummaging among the heaps of junk to find said item. When, under almost impossible circumstances, and after scaling the mountains of junk, they'd return empty handed, he'd become adamant that the item was there and that if it couldn't be found, then the boys must have either stolen or lost it. He reserved such occasions to trot out one of his favourite lines. "Do you think you can fool me?" This little gem was rivalled in its frequency of use only by his all time favourite of: "You won't be able to deceive me until you have hair coming out of your bottom!" There were small victories to be had though, and when Ginger's brother had neglected to lock the back door to the shop one night and a mangy old stray cat got in, it had made itself comfortable in the office and left a couple of itchy surprises in the form of fleas under the man's office desk!

Speaking of payback, his brother had also once gleefully recounted how he'd come close to killing the boy's tormentor. With the older boy's help, the man had been carrying out a television repair which had involved changing a valve close to the high tension box. Not really concentrating, Ginger's brother had been idly flicking the power switch on and off and at one point in the proceedings, he'd flicked the switch on while the man had his hand still stuck in the back of the set. The boy's actions sent a few thousand volts through the man, knocking him shouting, to the ground! Oblivious to what he had just done, Ginger's brother wondered why the hell he'd thrown himself onto the floor - 'mind you' he'd told the BIWB later; 'It may have earned me a slap, but it was worth it!'

The boy's mother had been full of ideas from which to try and make money and had been rather good at making things too. This enthusiasm for manufacturing was matched by the man's skill with wood and metal working and enriched by the fact that he literally had a ready-made shop front from which to display their efforts. Unfortunately for the boys, all manner of ongoing and half-finished projects meant that the man had virtually abandoned his failing television repair business in favour of setting up a workshop in the family home and with this, had come even longer periods of his dreaded presence at number 41. First came the shoe making business, which never really got beyond stretching various types of leather over wooden moulds, which now littered the house (the strip of polished hide used to punish the older boy with on the roof, had come from the doomed shoe project) The next pie in the sky idea was to begin making handbags; mainly made from shiny black patent leather, the clasps would be sourced from Valletta with the BIWB being despatched to collect them. In the end though, the handbags had gone the way of the shoes and their unfinished carcasses joined the same scrapheap as the unfinished shoes. Then there had been the attempt at dressmaking and accessorising. For the latter, the put upon boy would again be sent far and wide to source such items as the latest fashionable belts. These hadn't been belts in the practical sense of the word, but more of a decorative piece and had been made up of plastic hoops all linked together. The idea was, that they would be worn loosely around the waist with a surplus of rings dangling down and presumably distracting the eye of the beholder away from a plump waistline! The mainly male visitors to the man's shop however, had showed little interest in the latest women's styles, and the dresses and accompanying belts, went the way of the shoes and handbags. Then one day, a huge knitting machine – from goodness knows where - arrived at number 41. *Burda* magazines with their foldout knitting patterns became *en vogue* and the heady but temporary excitement of a new project reigned. Ginger had been despatched to the *Sirdar Wool* shop in Valletta to return with armfuls of wool – ultimately made into trial and error shapes, only to be consigned to the growing pile of wasted raw materials! One particularly impressive and adventurous project had been that of building from scratch, what was known back then as a "music centre" Utilising his electronic skills, the man had made an amplifier which he'd mounted onto a shaped piece of sheet metal. He'd punched holes into the square bridge-type mounting, in which to house the various valves, capacitors and brightly coloured resistors – again all collected from Valletta by the boy, who truth be known, had relished the opportunity to escape for a couple of hours. He'd been given bus fare, but would walk most of the way so as to pocket the fare and buy food. He'd always found Valletta to be an exciting place to visit…

The island's capital owes its existence to the Knights of St John, who planned the city as a refuge to care for injured soldiers and pilgrims during the Crusades in the 16th century. Until the arrival of the Knights, Mount Sceberras - on which Valletta stands - lying between two natural harbours, was no more than an arid tongue of land. No building stood on its bare rocks except for a small watchtower, called St Elmo, to be found at its extreme end. Grand Master La Valette, the hero of the Great Siege of 1565, soon realised that if the Order was to maintain its hold on Malta, it had to provide adequate defences. Therefore, he drew up a plan for a new fortified city on the Sceberras peninsula. Pope Pius V and Philip II of Spain showed interest in the project. They both promised financial aid and the Pope lent the Knights the services of Francesco Laparelli, a military engineer, who drew up the necessary plans for the new city and its defences. Work started in earnest in March 1566 - the year after the unsuccessful attempt at conquest by the Turks, and the new city was to be called Valletta in honour of Grandmaster La Valette, who'd orchestrated the gallant defence of the islands. The Grand Master hadn't lived to see its completion, dying in 1568. His successor, Pietro del Monte continued with the work at the same pace, and by 1571, the Knights had transferred their quarters from Vittoriosa (Birgu) to the new capital. Architect Laparelli left Malta in 1570 and was replaced by his assistant Gerolamo Cassar, who had spent some months in Rome, where he had observed the new style of buildings in the Italian city. Cassar designed and supervised most of the early buildings, including the Sacra Infermeria, St John's Church, the Magisterial Palace and the seven Auberges; or Inns of Residence of the Knights. By the 16th century, Valletta had grown into a sizeable city and people from all parts of the island had flocked to live within its safe fortifications - especially as Mdina, until then Malta's capital, had lost much of its lure. In the ensuing years, the austere mannerist style of Cassar's structures gave way to the more lavish palaces and churches with graceful facades and rich sculptural motifs. The new city, with its strong bastions and deep moats, became a bulwark of great strategic importance, with Valletta's street plan being unique and planned with defence in mind. Based on a more or less uniform grid, some of the streets fall steeply as you get closer to the tip of the peninsula. The stairs in some of the streets do not conform to normal dimensions since they were constructed in such a way, as to allow knights in heavy armour to be able to climb the steps. Several centuries later, the city had come under another siege; this time in the shape of World War II which brought havoc to Malta. Valletta was badly battered by the bombing, but the city withstood the terrible blow and, within a few years, it rose again. The scars of the war are still visible until this day – no more so than at the site previously occupied by the former Royal Opera House in the heart of the city which only now, after years of political wrangling, is being rebuilt in the style of a modern and open performing area. During the post-war years, Valletta lost many of its citizens who moved out to more modern houses in other locations, such as fashionable Sliema, and its population dwindled to less than 10,000 inhabitants.

The boy's favourite part of the city had been the Upper Barrakka Gardens. Created in 1821, on the bastions of Saint Peter and Paul, the gardens were originally the private garden of the Italian knights of the Order of Saint John. The gardens are the highest and most impressive point of the city walls, offering magnificent views of Sengles and Birgu, Fort Saint Angelo, Fort Ricasoli in Kalkara and the shipyard. In 1824, the gardens were opened to the public. Adorned with memorials to public figures past, high-ranking British naval and army officers dating back to British rule and even a dedication to Winston Churchill, its walls read like a history book of the islands. In the south-eastern corner there is a café and the remnants of a disused and basic cage-type lift, built by the Royal Engineers and opened in 1905. The lift had been built to take sailors and tourists down the vertiginous rock face to the harbour 180 feet below, so avoiding a long detour and countless steep steps. Standing at the entrance to the old lift, his sweaty hands gripping the rail and his stomach doing somersaults, the BIWB would look down, awestruck by the sheer drop. The people below appeared ant-like and the cars in the car park resembled toys. What had attracted the boy to the Barrakka, despite his fear of heights, had been the prospect of seeing part of his country's navy. There had usually been several warships at anchor in the harbour and sometimes aircraft carriers too; decks bristling with military hardware, seamen in starched uniforms and - if he were lucky, he'd get to see fighter aircraft on the deck. At the time of writing, the Maltese Government has undertaken a project to build another lift on the same site.

An old submariner had once told the boy a joke about sailors returning to their ships after a "run ashore" in Valletta. It had revolved around the commonly used taxis of the day, used by sailors to get back to their ships. The local name for these "taxis" had been *Karozzin;* which were covered horse drawn carriages, known to the sailors as *Garry* horses (a corruption of Gharry, from their counterparts in India and the Middle East) The old salt's story had gone something like this:

71

A sailor is late back to his ship after a run ashore. When brought before his commanding officer for an explanation, he states that he'd hired a Garry horse to bring him back, and on the way, the horse had dropped dead. Giving him the benefit of the doubt, the officer had the next latecomer wheeled in only to be presented with the same excuse. Several sailors with the same excuse later, the last offender had been brought before him. Putting a hand up to stop the forthcoming reason for the man's tardiness, he'd interjected with: 'Don't tell me – you were just on your way back when your Garry horse dropped dead?'

'No sir, I was on my way back to ship, but my driver couldn't get down the road for dead Garry horses!'

Chuckling over his own joke the submariner had left the ginger kid with a puzzling piece of advice – that should he ever be offered the chance to see a ship's "golden rivet" – particularly by the ship's cook - he should refuse!

The cabinet for the music centre had been a bold and futuristic design consisting of three rectangular plywood pods. The centre pod was to house the electronics and a turntable, while the other two – smaller and lower – would contain the loud speakers that would transmit in the new fangled stereophonic. The interior of the main pod had been finished in padded white plastic with a diamond shaped design. The turntable could be hidden and accessed by lifting a wooden lid that moved up and down by utilising a lockable sliding bracket. The cabinet had then been clad in sheets of *Formica,* which gave it a faux wood grain effect, and then buffed to a deep shine. Threaded housings were then screwed to the base into which long, splayed and simple legs were fitted. Apart from going off to collect electronic parts, the BIWB had been tasked to collect the raw materials for the construction of the cabinet from the timber yards that had been located at the bottom of the hill where Paola became Marsa Docks. This had been perhaps a distance of around a mile from number 41, but when laden down with timber and large sheets of plywood, which had dwarfed his small frame, it had seemed more like ten. The Egyptians invented plywood in around 3500 BC when the shortage of wood had necessitated the gluing of several thinner layers together to make one thick layer, but he history and ingenuity of the stuff was wasted on the boy as he'd lugged the wobbly eight-foot by four-foot sheets back up the hill to Valletta Road! The feat had required strength, tenacity and frequent stops in which to rest. If it had been a windy day, then it had taken all of his malnourished strength to prevent the sheets becoming sails and carrying him back down the hill from whence he'd come and into the murky water of the docks! In the event, due to the total lack of demand, only one of these music centres had been made, and it had taken pride of place at the man's shop from where - it had to be said - it was admired by passing trade, but never purchased. There, the manufacture of music centres – stereophonic or otherwise - had ended and another ambitious project had hit the buffers.

Marsa Docks had also been home to several metal work shops and foundries which back then, had serviced the needs of visiting ships, and it was to these workshops that the BIWB had been despatched to assist with the latest project: that of manufacturing fish aquariums. Cutting lengths of angle iron into the dimensions from which to fashion the aquariums, the man would send long-suffering Ginger to hang around the welding shops until, taking pity on the English boy, one of the workers would agree to weld the angle iron together into the desired shape. He'd spent hours watching the welders at work and could only thank them for their labours – provided free of course! Once the tanks had been welded into what would be the new home for guppies, black mollies and swordtails, he'd lug their not inconsiderable weight back up the hill to the waiting entrepreneur. The boy's next task would be that of visiting the local ironmonger and purchasing a sheet of glass, which much to the annoyance of the shopkeeper, had then to be cut into the correct sizes for the man's aquatic project! More juvenile donkeywork later and the man had simply to construct the tanks, by laying putty into the angle iron and fitting the glass. Needless to say, impoverished 1970's Malta had other priorities; which hadn't included buying homemade fish tanks, and apart from one retained by the boy's mother and filled courtesy of the Paola cobbler, the fish tank business had been consigned to the growing heap of entrepreneurial non-starters!

Actually, Marsa had been a regular haunt for the BIWB; it had been home to the local abattoir where he'd be sometimes sent to hang around (much like at the welders shop) in the hope that one of the butchers would hand him some unmentionable lump of waste meat, cut from the unfortunate animals and destined for either the glue factory or the dustbin. He'd hated being sent there; the smell of freshly butchered animals, the sound of bones being chopped and sawed, the noise of the killing bolts and the sight of gutted bovine carcasses swinging on their hooks, had upset him. If he'd been lucky, he'd be handed a couple of pig's trotters by some gruff but kindly butcher, which when taken home, would create another hated smell – that of the coarse hair being singed off over the gas cooker by his mother. He hadn't disliked all of the food forays he'd been sent on though, and the one thing that was not only free, but grew in abundance on the patch of waste ground at the bottom of his road, had been capers. He and his older brother had been sent for day-long caper picking sessions, and on that patch of waste ground, under the burning sun, they'd been able to escape the abuse and endless drudgery that was number 41.

Picking capers had felt therapeutic, and in between stripping the bushes of their succulent little buds, the boys had made the waste ground their playground. Also growing in abundance in their playground had been the cactus species *Opuntia* - or Paddle cactus - due to the shape of its leaves. Nobody really knew how the plant had got to the islands, but a native of Mexico, it hadn't been seen in Europe until after the discovery of the American continent. Grown as a windbreak in Malta and known for its succulent fruit – *Bajtar tax-xewk* in Maltese or simply *prickly pears* - the plant had provided two things for the English kids – food in the form of its spiny and seed-laden prickly pears; and an excellent victim of their boyish enthusiasm for sword fighting. Slashing the amazingly juicy paddle leaves with a length of wood, which in their minds had been a sword; the young vandals – aka Errol Flynn wannabes - had found the paddles to be very satisfying and easily defeated victims. When slashed, they'd oozed a lovely sticky liquid which although clear, had been a junior sword fighter's substitute for blood and gore! Another species to be found in large numbers on the waste ground had been geckos and a variety of lizards. If the boys had been stealthy and quick, they'd been able to sneak up on one of the basking reptiles and pounce on the unsuspecting creature, grabbing it by the tail. Not wanting to be an unwilling participant in Ginger's amateur school experiments – and most definitely wishing to avoid the frontal lobotomy - the lizards had mostly made good their escape by shedding their tails and scuttling off leaving the kid with a still twitching tail in his grubby little hand! Having failed to catch a lizard, the boys would turn their attention to the geckos, which in the heat of the Mediterranean afternoon, could be found clinging out of the boy's reach, to the stone walls that surrounded the waste ground. Observing the local kids, they'd fashioned catapults from "Y" shaped pieces of tree branch and old tyre inner tubes, and using these makeshift weapons, they had taken it in turns to try to hit and either knock the "minding their own business" geckos off the wall, or else squash them with a bloody splat against the stone! Once the haul of capers was taken home, they'd be washed, the surplus stems removed one by one, and then put into vinegar-filled jars before being taken up onto the roof and joining the other several dozen oversized jars of capers already stored there, in various stages of pickling. The boys had never really known why they'd been sent out to pick capers; after all, how many of the damn things could one family eat? It may have been an exercise in getting rid of them for the day, but it had remained a mystery. On the few occasions when the BIWB had enjoyed some down time, he'd inevitably headed for Marsa Docks, where he'd fished for mullet. One such day while, admiring the polished hull of a visiting yacht, the boy had been thrilled to see a shoal of tiny seahorses, their curly tails and gossamer fins propelling them gracefully around it. Using a crudely constructed line with lead shot, a wine bottle cork and a hook, he'd walked across the flat barges used for the transportation of coal and when he'd been several barge widths from the dock, he'd pressed sodden, mouldy bread around his hook and settled down under the sun to observe the cork. His success with mullet catching hadn't exactly been record-breaking; in fact the sum of his haul had usually consisted of the odd inedible dogfish dragged from out of the depths of the oily dock water. The "one that *didn't* get away" notwithstanding, he'd taken the opportunity to indulge in some human contact while in Marsa, in the form of the older fishermen, who he'd badgered with such inane questions as "caught anything yet?" Examining his fellow fishermen's catch languishing in their cloth-covered buckets and resigned to being ignored by them, he'd wind up his line and head to the nearest bar with an owner foolish enough to leave his stock of empty bottles unattended, where he'd go through the ritual of cashing in empties in exchange for food or cigarettes.

Eventually, the only member of the household to have been bringing in a wage – albeit a meagre one - to number 41, had been the boy's older brother. He'd secured an early morning job with a local newsagent (Carrabott) in Paola's main square. The BIWB hadn't known it at the time, but it later transpired that his brother had artfully hidden the actual amount that he'd earned from the man. As a result, he'd concocted an ingenious plan to introduce the surplus cash to Ginger in the form of the following ruse: There had been an area close to the boy's home known between them as the "triangle of trees" This had been a recreational area fitted out with wooden benches where the old men of the village would while away the twilight hours, and kids would play. The area had been triangular in shape and had been bounded by trees planted in circular concrete pits, not quite flush with the ground. The boy's older brother would, from time to time, engineer a walk to the triangle of trees, where walking slightly ahead of his gullible sibling, he would drop money into the concrete tree planters, before exclaiming: 'I've found some money!' This had been his way of justifying to the inquisitive boy how he'd come to have the money hidden from the all-seeing man! The older boy would stash his money under his pillow, and by giving the odd titbit to his brother, he'd avoid detection. The unintended product of his brother's subterfuge, had been Ginger's frequent trips to the triangle of trees in search of the El Dorado which had simply never existed! After some time, the older boy had accrued enough spare cash to buy himself not only fashionable clothes, but he'd actually saved up enough money to buy a gleaming gold-coloured three speed bicycle with the amazing and exciting addition of a speedometer which read all the way up to forty miles per hour!

Not long after the slight of hand that had been the triangle of trees, Ginger's brother, had got himself a job pumping gas at the same station where as younger kids, they'd run errands for the attendants. The job had been comparatively well paid and he'd become quite independent from the misery at number 41. By British standards of the day, he'd been too young to work full time, but Maltese law of the early 1970's had allowed him to do so. The ability to work full time, had eventually brought him to the notice of the authorities, who'd soon realised that he hadn't officially existed. On that basis, he'd been unable to obtain a work permit and he'd been forced to leave the country. Through a contact he'd managed to secure a job in London as a furrier and with that, his Maltese odyssey had come to an end and a new life back in the country of his birth had begun. At the fur factory, he'd earned the princely sum of eighteen pounds a week. The tentacles of his mother's Maltese lover, however, had extended the sixteen hundred and twenty miles, from sunny Malta to snowy London, and it was demanded that he contribute half of his weekly wage to the cause of the rest of the family. In reality, this had meant that the boy's brother spent half of his paltry wages on food and accommodation and sent the other half, back to Malta. This enforced arrangement meant that he didn't have enough money with which to travel to work, leaving him with no choice but to wake at four in the morning to enable him to walk the seven miles to work. At the end of his shift, he'd have to walk back home again to his miserable bedsitting room. Meanwhile, the money he sent home would be added to the monthly alimony cheque sent by his father, long since bereft of his family. At around this time, the BIWB had also been expected to contribute financially to the family coffers, and a pre-school job with an eye-wateringly early start time, had been arranged at the bakery on the edge of the waste ground. The only consolation to the ridiculously early starts had presented itself in the form of the daughter of the bakery owner. The girl's voluptuous form, clad in a denim mini-skirt, had provided the boy with all manner of teenage fantasies! His duties had included drawing sweet tasting water from the bakery's well, and accompanying the delivery van on its early morning rounds. On a Sunday, he'd helped with the baking of Sunday dinners, brought by local people who didn't have access to an oven. Delivered in metal trays to be cooked inside the baker's cavernous oven, the dinners would later be collected by the local women who would identify their roast dinners by means of the metal discs issued to them by the baker when they'd arrived with their trays.

At around this time, the boy's mother, who was already skilled in the use of watercolours, had begun to experiment with oil painting. She'd been quite an accomplished artist and her first large scale painting had depicted a scene from her favourite ballet *Swan Lake*. A romantic at heart, her painting had depicted her version of the pas de deux of Prince Siegfried and Odette with a string of dancers in the background; all painted on hardboard left over from the back cover of the music centre. After this she'd gone on to paint an English village scene in which two head-scarved women chatted as they ambled along a country lane. The boy's mother became a prolific painter and began to paint the walls of number 41, decorating them with tall willowy trees and flowers. In doing so, she'd created the impression of wallpaper; something she'd not seen since leaving Britain. Her desire to paint had created even more Valletta trips for the boy, where he'd been sent to the only Winsor and Newton oil paint stockist on the island. The world of *Burnt Sienna, Cobalt Violet, Prussian Green, Winton Hog* brushes and charcoal sticks, had soon become his vernacular, and had fed the creative nature of a woman far from home, held for so long in virtual captivity. For his part, her loving incarcerator had moved on to his next scheme: that of entering politics. Putting himself forward as contender for selection as local Member of Parliament for the Labour Party, he'd hopelessly squandered part of the scarce family income on large publicity photos of himself to be plastered around Paola. In the event, he never managed to garner enough votes to be selected and had cried foul, alleging that the voting had been rigged against him. With that, he appeared to give up on all the bright money making ideas, and immersed himself in cheap wine and self-pity. The failed business man-cum-politician achieved one success – that of impregnating his English lover and nine months later, having lost one son who had departed for London, the boy's mother had gained another…

Chapter Six
Under The Knife
'Do you think he'll be alright?'

The first time the BIWB had suspected something had been wrong with his mum, had been when he'd come across her sobbing in the dining room. He'd known her to cry on many other occasions, normally after the man had left for the night; like the time she'd been crying after being accused of goodness knows what after Vladi's friend the drum banger's visit. This time, she'd fobbed him off with a story about how she'd heard a sad song about a rose on the radio, which had made her cry, but the boy hadn't been convinced; her sorrow was tangible. His mother had begun to spend more and more time in bed; leaving him to take care of the day to day running of the house, looking after his new brother, washing nappies and doing the ironing. Whenever the man had been in the house, him and the boy's mother had spent most of their time cooped up in the bedroom with their child. The bedroom had been generally out of bounds to the boy, and sometimes, he'd spent an age with his ear pressed to the cool glass paneled door, straining to determine whether his mother had been alone inside that forbidden chamber. Every now and then, he would be summoned to complete some chore or another, when after knocking, he'd enter to be given his task. One day, he'd been called and gone into the room to find his mum lying in the darkened room with several sliced potatoes arranged across her forehead. This bizarre scene, it seemed, had been created by the man whose remedy for her fever had been to cool her brow with slices of raw potato! Back then, a British weekly magazine edited by Richard Cavendish with the title of *Man Myth and Magic* had arrived on the scene and very quickly attracted a cult following among who, were the boy's mother and the man. The magazine was an encyclopedia of the supernatural including magic, mythology and religion. The periodical, with its articles on black magic, voodoo, weird and wonderful beliefs garnered from around the globe and featuring hideous illustrations; had become an obsession for the man, and the BIWB would be sent to the newsagents every week to collect a copy. At the time, this hadn't meant all that much to the boy, but when he'd begun to be regularly given letters to post to mysterious and exotic sounding names in equally exotic eastern countries, he'd started to wonder what was going on. Compounded by this, had been the conversation he'd heard one morning while, ear pressed up against the bedroom door, he'd heard the man talking of a mystic he'd heard about who could make a hen's egg spin just by looking at it! Speaking of eggs, the man had begun to feed the boy's mother a daily concoction of raw eggs, beaten in a tumbler with a dash of Scotch which, grimacing, she'd dutifully swallowed.

Some weeks before, the family chicken – Brenda had seemed like she'd been on her last legs, and the kid's mum had tried to treat the stricken hen with a daily dose of Scotch; Brenda, buoyed temporarily - no doubt by the sudden intake of alcohol shoved down her beak – had rallied for a few days before dropping dead either from whatever had been ailing the poor bird, or alcoholic poisoning! It seemed that treatment with Scotch; however futile, had been in vogue at number 41!

The boy's mother got religion around this time; converting to Catholicism, festooning her newborn baby with religious medals pinned to his vests, and developing a fascination with the Virgin Mary. Ginger, feeling mischievous had decided to wind her up by suddenly exclaiming loudly: 'Santa Maria!' He'd intended it to sound like a traditional Maltese outburst - he'd heard the way the locals had sworn and it had mostly involved cursing some religious deity or other or even the Holy Host. To avoid his newly religious mother's wrath at hearing her son utter the name of a saint, he'd devised a cunning plan which involved the hasty explanation that *Santa Maria* had been the name of one of the ships sailed in by Christopher Columbus, and having learned all about this at school, he'd been merely repeating the name of the ship and not swearing! Ginger's mum hadn't fallen for this subterfuge and had ordered him to drink a glass of water laden with salt to cleanse his rotten blasphemous mouth! To coincide with this religious fervour, the man decided that from this time on, the BIWB should go to mass at the local church (Ta'Lourdes) every single day. The first mass was at

6am and then hourly after that until 9am. The man had thought it a great idea if the boy were to attend the 6am mass, which would not only coincide with his arrival at number 41, but also allow the English kid to have time after mass to wash the floors before going to school. By this time, Ginger's "bedroom" had consisted of the space under the stairs at the end of the hallway; just tucked out of sight of the front door to the house. His bed had been a grotty old horsehair mattress and blood spattered walls - the result of squashed mosquitoes - were his decorations. No teenage posters for company, just bare sandstone walls with the odd nighttime gecko competing for space with the moths and mosquitoes. Every morning the BIWB had been woken from his fitful sleep by the sound of a key in the door followed by the man's click-clacking iron-shod shoes, as he walked towards the stairs wreathed in the blue smoke of his second cheap cigarette of the day. Pausing only to tell the boy to get up and go to church - or he'd return with a bucket of water to throw over him - the man would ascend the stone steps and enter the boy's mother's bedroom, from where he'd continue to issue orders to the reluctant churchgoer.

The BIWB, must have been the only non-Catholic to have attended *Ta'Lourdes* and he never knew how it had all been arranged; but so impressed had the priest been with the boy's (forced) regular attendance, he'd soon elevated *L-Ingliz* to the lofty position of altar boy. Not only did he get to assist the priest with mass, but later, he would get to be one of the bell ringers too! Unfortunately for the BIWB, such "dedication" soon included having to assist with evening rosary recital. Basically, this was attended by the older women of the village, who, having attended mass that morning, would now give their confessions to the priest before the incantation of the rosary. Those ladies must have been totally purged of all sin! - After all, their confessions had consisted of relating to the patient priest behind the curtain, every facet of their day, every bad thought and perceived ungodly deeds since the last time they had seen the unfortunate man since morning mass! Inevitably, the BIWB couldn't hope to escape conversion to Catholicism forever, after all, an altar boy christened in the church of England, simply couldn't continue to serve at the altar, and arrangements were made for *L-Ingliz* to take his first Holy Communion. Actually, since he'd attended Ta'Lourdes, the boy had taken communion with the rest of the faithful, and what's more, he'd done so after confession, as was the rule. The only problem with "confessing" had been, that Ginger never really knew what to confess *to*. After consulting with his fellow altar boys, he'd simply invented a couple of "sins" and gone off to recite his penance of how ever many Hail Marys the priest saw fit to award him! Another of the boy's ecclesiastical duties had been that of accompanying the parish priest on his daily visits to his parishioners around the village. Crammed into the passenger seat of the holy man's wheezing old Fiat 500, the ginger altar boy had had the dubious pleasure of assisting the priest during his rounds of the sick, housebound, and those at death's door. For the latter group, the BIWB had listened as blessings and prayers were accompanied by the wheedling exhortations that: should they see fit to leave a "little something" to the church in their wills, the almighty would surely show them favour in the afterlife!

When the day of the English kid's First Holy Communion arrived; in contrast to his peers, who had all been accompanied by proud family members, he'd been alone. The priest, who he'd assisted at the altar every day, had been an unusually enlightened man and less than an hour before the ceremony had taken place, he'd done something no adult had ever done before – he'd given the boy a choice. The priest had taken his altar boy to one side, and placing a fatherly hand on his shoulder, he'd asked the BIWB whether he was sure he wanted to go ahead with it. Truth be known, the kid hadn't really thought about it; he had been almost indifferent as to whether he took the first step to becoming a Catholic or not. Thing was though, presented with a choice for what seemed the first time in his young life, the boy had told the kindly priest – just for the hell of it – that he didn't want to proceed! There hadn't been any fuss and no more had been said about his refusal. He'd continued to serve as altar boy and bell ringer at Ta'Lourdes and simply gone back home neglecting to mention to the man and his newly religious lover that he'd not gone through with it!

One evening, the hated man, had inexplicably left much earlier than had been his habit and the boy, along with his younger brother, had got to spend precious time with their mother. Sitting them down with her at the dining room table, she'd told her children that she'd been ill. She'd glossed over the details, but suffice to say, she was soon to leave the island to seek treatment in London with a specialist, as the local doctors back then hadn't been equipped to deal with her "condition" She'd been on form, just like their pre-incarceration mother of old. She'd been tactile and loving on that evening - laughing and joking with her boys about how she was "going under the knife" The BIWB sensed that their lives were about to change, he hadn't known why, but whatever was wrong with his mother, he'd been sure it had been more grave than she had been bravely suggesting. She'd diverted the boy's attention by theatrically reenacting the illustrations from the *Teach Yourself Karate* book of torn out pages fame; performing karate chops, and wheeling around the room while mimicking the karate masters cries and shouts. This had been the last time the BIWB had seen his mother as he'd known and loved her, and a few days after her martial arts performance, she'd boarded an aircraft and set off on a last chance visit to the home of her birth, where she was to be operated on in an attempt to diagnose and treat her illness. The man had later joined her on her trip, but before that, in London; she'd met up with the boy's older brother. Tragically, in seeking accommodation for her in grim 1970's Kings Cross in London; her and her eldest son had suffered the ignominy of been turned away from several bed and breakfast establishments, the proprietors of which; used to the vice trade rife in the area at the time, had mistaken them for a prostitute and her client before refusing them entry.

The boy's mother was never set to foot in number 41 again and the first the boy knew of the actual gravity of her condition, had been the return of the man. He'd callously informed the boy that his mother had been diagnosed with the latter stages of terminal ovarian cancer. Continuing that his mother had been admitted straight into Saint Lukes Hospital – ironically in Pieta, where the family's Maltese odyssey had begun - he'd showed the kid the consultant's letter brought back from the hospital in

London. The letter had been written in medical jargon, but the boy had understood the parts that described his mother's liver and other internal organs as being grossly enlarged and there, dictated by a surgeon to his secretary, were the words which starkly suggested that there was no hope of his mother ever recovering. Just like the time when he'd quoted the dictionary definition of "bastard" which had so enraged the man, the boy researched ovarian cancer and its causes before spitefully suggesting to the grief-stricken man, that one of the causes of cancer in that region was the result of a rough and violent birth. The man hadn't reacted in the way that the boy had hoped with his barely concealed reference to his half brother's birth; he'd simply looked puzzled and remarked that his son had "come out like a cake"

Not long after his mother's return to Malta, the boy had gone alone to Saint Lukes to visit his mum. He hadn't seen her for a few weeks and her appearance had shocked him. Lying in her bed with the pull-up gated sides preventing her from falling out, she was a pitiful sight. Ravaged by massive doses of futile chemotherapy, her once full and attractive face was gaunt; her thinned hair, attacked by radiation and in places revealing her gleaming scalp, was glued in pathetic wispy strands to her sweaty forehead. Her laboured breathing was ragged and came in gasps as she opened her hooded eyes to look wearily at her son. Clearing her catarrh-laden throat, robbed of even the dignity to swallow, she spat out chunks of green phlegm onto a tissue. Taking in her skeletal body, the boy held her hand and gently swabbed her dry and cracked lips with the lemon-flavoured cotton buds left by her bedside. The boy was devastated - just weeks before, she'd been bouncing around the dining room of number 41 chopping the air and kicking in the style of a karate grandmaster and now here she was, no more than a pathetic sack of wheezing bones. Gripping the boy's hand in what had been reduced to a bony claw, the stricken woman had made him promise to look after his baby brother. Anxious to grant his sick mother anything she'd wanted; if only to make her feel a bit better, he'd vigorously agreed to make sure that his brother – son of his mother and the man - would be

85

well looked after. Returning her weak smile, he'd moistened her lips once more before leaving the hospital and returning home.

The BIWB had been woken from a fitful sleep on his mattress under the stairs, by the familiar and hated click clacking of the man's shoes on the tiled hall floor. Pausing at the bottom of the stairs, cigarette in hand; without even addressing the boy face to face, he'd simply announced: 'She's gone' before mounting the rest of the steps. This had been the cold and uncaring way in which the boy had found out that his mother had died. To be grudgingly fair, the man had been genuinely grieving, but true to form, this had taken the form of selfish self-indulgence, and the notion that the kid under the stairs had lost a mother at the age of 13, had been wasted on him. Later that miserable day, the man had suggested that the boy go to see his mother at the hospital, and making his way on the bus to Saint Lukes, he'd gone into reception where, after a short wait, he'd been greeted by two nurses. 'Was he sure he wanted to see his mum?' 'Yes' he'd answered, still numb from the news and not really sure how he'd felt. Leading the English kid into the depths of the old hospital, the nurses had paused at the door to the mortuary. He'd overheard the whispered question: 'Do you think he'll be alright?' whereupon shrugging, one of the nurses, pushing open the heavy plastic insulated doors to the morgue, had led the boy into the surreal world of the recently dead. The mortuary had seemed like a vast space to the kid; looking not unlike a warehouse, and the nurses had led him past rows of dead people; all laid out on slabs in their Sunday best. Passing an obese looking young boy dressed in his first Holy Communion suit, the boy heard one of the nurses tell the other that he'd died of a heart attack and finally, towards the end of that subterranean warehouse of the dead; there she was. Clad in an old, thin threadbare pink nightdress; which in days past had probably been her pride and joy, lay the boy's emaciated mother. Her nostrils stuffed with cotton wool to stem the flow of bodily fluids, she reposed, free from the shackles of her jealous lover and the pain which, hidden from her sons, had wracked her body for the last year of her life. Feeling the initial inability to display emotion common in male adolescence, the boy had walked right out of that awful place and returned home to an uncertain future – during which, he'd often wished he had spent longer at his dying mother's bedside…

Santa Maria Addolorata (Our Lady of Sorrows) Cemetery; designed by Emanuel Galizia and built between 1862 and 1868, sits on Tal-Horr Hill, Paola; just opposite the wasteland which had been the English kids' playground and had supplied the thousands of capers hand picked under the sun from the wild bushes. The largest and most beautifully designed cemetery in the country, it was built to serve the whole of Malta. Galizia had thoroughly researched English and European cemetery design before embarking on this huge and ambitious project. The entrance to the cemetery pointedly proclaims its neo-Gothicism, unexpected in largely Baroque Malta. The tall spire of the chapel is the first thing a visitor notices from afar, giving it ironically, the appearance of a British church. The gatehouse, complete with hexagonal battlemented tower, winged gargoyles, and pinnacles are reminiscent of Highgate cemetery in North London, which is also built on a hillside and it had been to this pine tree-strewn place of rest on a grey October morning in 1975, that the boy's mother had made her final journey.

The mourning party had been sparse; in keeping with a woman who, shackled to the gloomy interior of number 41, hadn't been given the chance of meeting people or making friends. Notable among the mourners, had been Antonia – the Ginger Lady. Once the hearse had discharged the emaciated remains of the once beautiful Englishwoman, the coffin had been carried towards the newly dug grave. Tucked away in a corner next to a stone wall, it had been a tricky manoeuvre manhandling the casket along the narrow path, but just a few yards from the grave, the man had hoarsely and without warning, commanded the bearers to put the coffin down. Uncomprehendingly, they'd obeyed, and once they had put down the box containing the boy's mother's mortal remains, they and the accompanying mourners – the BIWB included – had watched in horror as the man, wild with grief, had thrown himself to his knees before clawing at the fastenings of the coffin lid. His horrified audience had watched in disbelief as, undoing the final fastening, he'd removed the lid, and with tears streaming down his cheeks, he had pressed his face to that of his decomposing lover, kissing her on her hard, cracked lips. His macabre outpouring of grief over, the man who once piloted the aircraft carrier of a Chevy around the narrow streets of Paola, stood as member of parliament and fleeced his customers, had risen to his feet and mercifully allowed the bearers to replace the lid. The dead woman's dignity restored, they'd picked up the coffin once more, shuffled the last few feet to the open grave and lowered the thirty-nine year old woman into her grave. For many weeks after his theatrical graveside performance, the man had repeatedly told the boy: 'I kissed her cold' and Ginger had hated the bastard even more, the man who had restricted his childhood access to his beloved mother, the tyrant who'd put an end to his climbing into his mother's bed, cuddling up to her and listening in wonder to her bedtime stories about the bear who loved *Fry's Chocolate Cream*; yes, he'd hated the bastard more than ever…

There hadn't been a headstone with which to commemorate the English woman's short and painful life – that wouldn't come for another twenty years. The only thing to mark the occasion, had been Antonia's amateur inscription of the date, carved into the soft stone covering the grave with the key to her front door. Returning to number 41, the boy and his brothers had more or less been left to their own devices. Due to the fact that he now had a young child – his flesh and blood to look after – the man began to spend more time at the house. When he hadn't been there, the BIWB had been in *loco parentis* - looking after his brother, washing diapers, ironing, cooking and later taking him to nursery. The man had withdrawn from everyday life and even the beatings had ceased, but what had brought him out of his mourning had been his latest business idea…

The boy's unofficial stepfather had neglected to inform the kid's father of the death of the airman's ex-wife, presumably fearing that this news may have affected the usual dispatch of the alimony cheque. With the monthly seventeen pounds being the only income with which to support the family now bereft of a mother, he'd come up with an idea to convert number 41 into a bed and breakfast guesthouse. The fact that he hadn't paid rent on the house for some time hadn't entered his conscience - as far as he'd been concerned, the place was his to do with as he pleased. His intended potential customers had been the Libyans and Chinese now flocking to the islands at the invitation of Labour's Dom Mintoff, who with the departure of the British, had been struggling to finance his left wing revolution. The Chinese, at that time under the leadership of Mao Zedong, had been more than happy to provide assistance to Malta. Geographically situated as it is in a most strategic position with a natural deep harbour, China, like many nations before it, had welcomed the chance to get a foothold in the region. The Turks had tried and failed; Napoleon had wrested the island from the knights in 1798, but had himself been ousted after an eventful two years by the British - who on the invitation of the Maltese, had driven the French from the islands and remained there from 1800 until 1964 when Malta had been granted independence.

In 1969, the then Captain Muammar Gaddafi, led a group of junior officers in a bloodless coup toppling King Idris of Libya. Declaring himself "colonel" he'd embarked upon his forty-year rule. Only 221 miles south of Malta with its new left wing government, Gaddafi had been quick to realise the potential of having Mintoff as an ally. Responding to the Labour government's appeal for assistance, he'd provided oil money to fund projects such as a desalination plant, mosques on the island for his countrymen and cheap fuel. It was said that later, after the bombing in 1986 of Gaddafi's complex by F111's of the USAF, Gaddafi had offered free oil to the Maltese in return for the use of a radar station left intact by the British. He reportedly sent his own operators to the island to refurbish and then man the radar. This would in effect, give him prior warning of any further attacks on Tripoli by the US. And so, 1975 saw the streets of Valletta thronging with Chinese – all dressed in identical drab Chairman Mao suits – and Libyan Arabs swathed head to toe in their uniform of Dishdasha. It had been the Libyans who the man had set his sights on wooing, and to whom, he'd intended to offer guesthouse accommodation at number 41…

In order to realise his rent-free vision of a bed and breakfast haven for visiting Arabs, the man had set about partitioning the larger rooms of the house into guest rooms. Sending the BIWB on numerous trips to Marsa Docks to collect endless sheets of chipboard and plywood, he'd enthusiastically embarked on his latest project. By this time, the boy had "inherited " his older brother's shiny racing bike - left behind when he'd relocated to London. Hatching a plan that would enable the boy to transport even heavier loads from the docks for his project, the man had constructed a cart that could be harnessed to the bicycle. Resembling a cart traditionally pulled by a horse and coupled by braided nylon rope to the bike's frame, it had long wooden-handled shafts and a carriage running on large pram-type wheels. A closely slatted base completed the cart, upon which various loads could be hauled. When he hadn't been hauling timber and other construction materials, the boy had been sent to the island's airport (Luqa) where he'd been expected to tout for business among the arriving Arabs. He'd hated this task, and hadn't really put much effort into drumming up custom. Needless to say, the oil-rich Libyans had looked down their aquiline noses at the scruffy urchin of a boy, and at best had ignored his unenthusiastic advances, setting the guest house venture on the road to doom and consigning it to the same fate of all the other business ideas hatched at number 41.

Shortly after the man had hitched the cart to the bike, the boy had sped everywhere on it, and going downhill – according to the speedometer - he'd reached 40MPH! He'd watched other kids on their bikes who, waiting until the ancient buses grinding their way up the hill to his village, had stopped at a bus stop, they'd first make sure they were out of the driver's view, before grabbing hold of the ornate chrome rear fender and hitching a lift up the hill. With a new cycling speed record in mind, the BIWB had decided to better the boys who he'd seen being towed *up* the hill. His record-breaking plan had involved lying in wait for a bus traveling *downhill* to Marsa Docks. That way, he'd figured he'd get the speedo reading right off the clock! When after a short wait, no buses had appeared, he'd grown impatient to put his theory into action and had cycled up to a big truck which had slowed down to negotiate the roundabout. Grabbing hold of the fender, he'd been whizzed down the hill at speeds of up to 50MPH! His plan had been to let go of the truck just as it passed the junction with a quiet road on his left, before freewheeling to a stop. Unfortunately, having been so close to the back of the hurtling truck, he'd failed to see the left hand signal light indicating that the driver also planned to turn left! Boy and truck had made the turn together, resulting in the rapid narrowing of the gap between boy, bike and the stone wall on his left. Panic made Ginger's fingers refuse to obey his brain which was screaming 'Let go of the fuckin' fender you idiot!' Whether the driver saw his unexpected tow and slowed right down, or whether he'd just slowed for the corner, the boy hadn't known, but even the sudden decrease in speed hadn't prevented Ginger and his brother's gleaming bike becoming a terrified sandwich between wall and truck. How he'd escaped with only cuts and bruises only the good Lord knew, but the bike had become a twisted wreck and wouldn't be hauling loads of wood for the man's bed and breakfast project ever again! Luckily the shocked driver had been sympathetic and no doubt relieved that he hadn't killed the kid and so, putting a friendly arm around the boy, he'd helped him up into his cab, chucked the pile of scrap that had been his brother's bike into the back of the tipper, and driven Ginger back up the hill to Valletta Road, to face the wrath of the man!

Eventually, realising that Catholicism and Communism mix with the ease of oil and water, the Chinese had withdrawn from Malta leaving behind an impressive collection of gigantic dockyard cranes and general infrastructure. The Libyans had retained their presence on the island, but besides the island's strategic position, there hadn't been much to attract the numbers that had first arrived, and the arrangement of cooperation, an exchange of labour, cheap oil and other subsidised goods was all that had remained. None of the political shenanigans had been of any consequence to the BIWB when a short time into his position as inept lead salesman for the guesthouse on Valletta Road, he'd had a chance encounter which was to change his life forever…

Part Three

Chapter Seven
A New Beginning Out Of The Sun
'Unaccompanied Minors'

Marsaxlokk Bay can be found on the south east coast of Malta. Its name originates from two words spliced into one – Marsa – the Arabic word for harbour or port – and sirocco, from the Italian for southeast, which is the way the bay faces. Throughout history, Marsaxlokk has been strategically important with various historic buildings remaining as proof. One of the oldest historic features is Ghar Dalam. Translating as "dark cave", it is a prehistoric cul-de-sac found to contain the bone remains of animals that had become stranded and subsequently extinct on Malta at the end of the ice age. Nearby is a Bronze Age fortified settlement - Borg In-Nadur, a pre-historic temple of Hercules, and a Medieval Chapel (Tas-Silg) The earliest description of Marsaxlokk is provided by Jean Quintin D'Autun who also refers to the Bay as the Port of Hercules. In May 1565, the Turks moored their naval force in the bay, which would later cause the Knights to perceive the strategic importance of Marsaxlokk, and once the Turks had been routed, they invested huge amounts of money into the building of fortifications all around the bay. In 1798, when Napoleon took over Malta, he moored his navy in Marsaxlokk since it was the largest bay and offered less resistance than the Grand Harbour. Once the British had sent Napoleon packing, they too had invested heavily in the defence of the harbour. More recently in 1989, the historical importance of the bay was recognised when President Bush attended a Summit Meeting with the then Soviet Chairman, Mikhail Gorbachev. Marsaxlokk was to be instrumental in the writing of a bit more history – that of the BIWB...

Fourteen years before the cold war giants had met to thrash out yet another arms treaty, the BIWB; oblivious to the history of Marsaxlokk, had trudged his way there along the dusty roads from Paola. He'd been in search of a rarity on the islands – that of an English school friend who he knew to live in the village. He'd not told the man where he was going, and in need of a friendly face and some respite from his hated daily trips to the airport, he'd disobeyed his dead mother's lover who'd sent him off on yet another unfruitful journey to hand out bed and breakfast cards to disinterested Arabs. Stopping at a house on a side street leading to the bay, he'd knocked on the door of his friend only to get no reply. Disappointed and about to walk the three miles back to Valletta Road, he'd been surprised to find himself being addressed in English by an eccentric looking middle-aged lady who'd popped out from a house two doors down. The boy's friend, she'd explained, had returned to England, but equally eager for some English company, the lady had invited the boy into her house. The woman hadn't quite lived alone; she'd shared her home with a huge hairy Alsatian dog called Grimm. Nervous from his earlier terrifying encounter with dogs, the boy had soon been reassured when he realised all the languid hound had wanted to do, had been to sniff at the new arrival before retiring disinterestedly to resume its position at the feet of his mistress.

Ginger's newfound friend, in her apparent loneliness and isolation, had taken to drinking in the afternoon, and after a brief interrogation of his circumstances, she'd announced that they were going into the village to get a drink. Feeling very grown up and buoyed by her much needed company, he'd happily agreed and walked with her to her favourite seafront bar. Along the way, they'd passed a kind of washhouse, which looking like a giant well under a metal canopy, had been filled with seawater flowing straight in from the bay. Clustered around this covered well, had been a gaggle of chattering housewives, young and old, all scrubbing their family's weekly laundry, using big cakes of soap and large scrubbing brushes. Pounding the clothing on the sides of the well, the women finished off their routine by rinsing them under the constantly circulating seawater before taking the laundry home to dry on sun-bleached rooftops.

Sitting on the seafront drinking the same drink as her (gin and tonic) and feeling at ease in her presence, he'd poured out his story to the lady with the dog. Visibly moved by the scrawny kid's miserable tale, she'd insisted he stay with her while she made contact with an old friend from the British High

Commission in Floriana. Happy to stay away from the man, his bed and breakfast, scornful Libyans and his horsehair mattress underneath the stairs; the BIWB had agreed on the spot. A couple of days later, he'd met another kindly lady - Mrs. Goldsmith from the British High Commission. Appalled by the boy's plight, she'd arranged a meeting at the embassy, and later, standing in the foyer of the air conditioned splendour of what remained of colonial Britain, he'd been ushered in for an interview with Mrs. Goldsmith's superior. The officials at the embassy had tracked down the boy's long-lost father who, having had no idea of the demise of his ex-wife, agreed to pay the airfare of the boy and his brother so that they could return to Britain. For one reason or another - possibly because the boy had outstayed his welcome in Marsaxlokk after an innocent remark about the lady's dog Grimm being smelly - alternative arrangements had been made for him to stay elsewhere until his repatriation. Behind the scenes, embassy staff had made contact with Father Valente; the rector from Mount Carmel College and he'd agreed to help with temporarily housing the boys.

Mount Carmel College in Santa Venera had been tacked onto a Carmelite monastery and its chapel. The monks, at the request of Father Valente, had generously thrown open their monastery to the English kid and admitted him into their tranquil home. It was doubtful whether in the history of the place, it had ever opened its doors to the likes of the BIWB before! Given a comfortable and airy room of his own – a million miles from his mosquito infested bed space back at number 41, the boy had lapped up the attention afforded him by the curious and bemused monks. Sitting on the hard wooden refectory benches, he'd attended regular meals and when he'd compared his life to what it had been just one week before; he'd felt as though he were now in the lap luxury. In order to cement his new feeling of freedom, he'd somehow managed to get hold of a cigar that when shoved into his mouth, had dwarfed his freckly little face! Filling his room with clouds of blue smoke, he'd just started puffing away on his triumphant smoke, when a monk had tapped at his door to call him down to dinner. Poking his head around the door, he'd taken in the sight of the skinny English kid smoking a large and very adult cigar! Smiling benignly, the monk had gently closed the door and made his way back down to the refectory.

The boy's next moment of triumph had been when Father Valente had informed him that the man, who'd traveled from Paola, had been downstairs and was demanding to see his errant bed and breakfast sales boy. Just like the priest at the Ta'Lourdes church some months before, Father Valente had given the boy a choice – this time, that of seeing the man or sending him away. Taking control of his life for the second time that year, the BIWB had gleefully announced that he wouldn't see the man, and the spluttering tyrant had been sent back to Valletta Road cursing the ginger kid who'd dared to stand up to him. Thanks to his chance encounter with the kindly lady in Marsaxlokk, the warmth and concern of Mrs. Goldsmith and the support of the wonderful Father Valente, the BIWB - *L'Ingliz*, had been given back his name - the surname that had been taboo for all the years that he'd inhabited number 41...

After a short stay with the hospitable Carmelite monks of Santa Venera, the boy's younger brother arrived at the monastery and within a week the boys had been delivered to Luqa airport by embassy staff and escorted aboard a British European Airways aircraft for their journey back to Britain. Wearing clothes supplied to them by the High Commission, the boys wore metal badges on their shirts denoting them as "Unaccompanied Minors" and a short time into the flight, the BIWB, feeling very pleased with himself, had discovered the button with which to summon the smiling and attractive stewardess. Without batting an eyelid, the older of the unaccompanied minors had confidently asked the amused stewardess for a can of beer. She'd played along, and as he'd sipped the cold lager, he'd brazenly lit up a cigarette and contentedly sat back to enjoy the flight. As the muted roar of the plane's jet engines carried the boys back home, they weren't to know that the country they were about to be reacquainted with, had been going through turmoil of a much greater magnitude than the one they had recently left. Ironically, also under a Labour government such as the one back on Malta, Britain was crippled by industrial action - three-day weeks, a devalued currency and rampant unemployment. Labeled "The Sick Man of Europe" by the rest of the continent, the Labour government had, in desperation, applied to the IMF for a £2.3 billion loan; this is the equivalent of £13 billion today. The boy's country of birth was also engaging in what had been known as the "cod wars" with British and Icelandic gunboats confronting each other over fishing rights, and the punk band, *The Sex Pistols* were riding high on the rising popularity of anarchy. In that year, the Notting Hill Carnival erupted in riots with 100 police officers injured along with 60 revelers. In Northern Ireland, Catholics and Protestants were slaughtering each other with monotonous regularity and the IRA were planting bombs on mainland Britain bringing chaos to its cities. On a more positive note, the first supersonic airliner - Concorde (a collaboration between France and Britain), made its first commercial flight, and that summer, a rare heat wave - to rival the Maltese summers the boy had known in Malta – had struck the country. This had brought drought and standpipes onto the streets, but totally used to such heat, the BIWB hadn't understood what all the fuss had been about. He hadn't known of course, that Libya hadn't had the courtesy to install a desalination plant like the one Gaddafi had back on Malta.

Arriving back to an England in the grip of winter, the boys had been met at London Heathrow airport by their older brother, who'd been mid-way through a week of night shifts at a bakery in London. He'd spent two days at the airport in that quasi-conscious state of a night worker waiting for his brothers who, for one reason or another hadn't arrived on time. Touching down late and only just managing to board the last train from Kings Cross to Lincoln, they'd traveled as far as Grantham where they'd been met by a social worker – Mr. "M" and transferred to his car for the onward journey to Lincoln. The flight and illicit lager had made the boy drowsy and he'd sat in the back with his kid brother watching the frozen landscape slip by. After what seemed like an age, they arrived in the city of Lincoln; home to the boy's maternal grandparents and his great-grandfather (to whom the house opposite Lincoln's prison belonged.) The boy hadn't been privy to the arrangements made for him by social services and so had assumed that he would be staying with his mother's parents on a permanent basis. His grandmother had been much as he'd remembered her, all bonhomie and cigarette ash, but his grandfather, of the "hiding behind the door and jumping out at him" fame, had been more subdued, surly and unwelcoming even. One thing that hadn't changed had been the ritual sitting down at four-thirty on a Saturday afternoon to watch the wrestling, just as they'd done back in Wolverhampton, and there in his grandparent's house, he'd joined his older brother and his Gran in cheering on their heroes such as *Big Daddy*, and booing the villains like *Giant Haystacks*. His great-grandfather, who he'd no recollection of ever meeting, had been well into his nineties by then and although in full possession of his faculties, the old man had relied on his son to tend to those bodily needs he could no longer manage alone; such as shaving. His first words, when coming down the stairs in the morning had inevitably referred to his toilet habits, and success on the "throne" was normally followed by the triumphant announcement to all and sundry, that he'd: "had a good move"

Once in Lincoln, he'd met his grandmother's three sisters. There had been the spinster who'd lived quietly in religious piety, who the BIWB had once visited and sat in her front room where she'd not uttered more than two words. After a couple of hours with the silence only broken, quite literally by the ticking of the clock on his great-aunt's mantelpiece, he'd given up on discovering that particular part of his maternal family tree – not to mention giving up on the earlier held prospect of a financial handout! He'd seen a bit more of the second of his grandmother's sisters, a lovely old girl with twinkling eyes and a penchant for bingo, which she'd indulged once a week with her cigarette-smoking sister. The boy would sometimes meet up with them both when they went for their other weekly treat - that of a posh milky coffee in a department store in Lincoln. As for the third sister; she'd spent a good deal of her life also dedicated to the church, but in her case, she'd taken God's word and spread it as a missionary in Africa. The boy had only met her once, when she'd returned home from Africa and had been invited to dinner at 77 Greetwell Road. She'd startled him with her random cries of 'Hallelujah!' and 'Praise the Lord!' At the dinner table, she'd led the saying of grace topped off with even more "Hallelujah's!" on her final return from Africa, she'd gone on to become a deaconess who celebrated mass in Lincoln's iconic cathedral. The boy had been amused and not a little taken aback, when after the meal in such hallowed company, his great-grandfather had whipped out his dentures, placed them onto the pristine Sunday best tablecloth, and proceeded to prise out the food caught in them, using his dinner knife! No stranger to courting controversy or bowing to the sensibilities of others, he'd once hung dead pigs to cure in his son's bedroom!

Once installed in the house at Greetwell Road, the boys had enjoyed a honeymoon period during which time, they'd re-acquainted themselves with their older brother and explored their new snowbound home. Accustomed to being put to work to earn their meagre keep back in Malta, the boy had asked his grandmother whether she had wanted her floors washing; of course, back in Britain, there had been no need for cool tiled floors, and as for the carpets: 'No, duck', she'd chuckled. 'There's a vacuum cleaner for that!' Shortly after the boy's arrival, his grandmother had received a letter from the Archbishop's office in Malta. It had been a sympathetic letter, acknowledging the suffering their mother had gone through and stating that they had arranged for them to attend the local Catholic school of Saint Peter and Saint Paul's. About the same time as that of the Archbishop's, another more sinister letter had arrived. It had been addressed to the boy and bore a Maltese stamp. Sitting in his grandparent's back room next to the roaring coal fire, the boy had ripped open the envelope to reveal a short note written in the unmistakable slanting hand of the Maltese man. Referring to the promise the boy had made to his dying mother the last time he'd seen her alive, the spiteful note had simply read: "*You have deceived your mother.*" He'd assumed that what the man back in Paola had meant by this was the fact that he had fled the island, effectively abandoning his brother and therefore breaking the promise he'd made to his mother. Ginger had screwed the nasty little missive into a ball and hurled it onto his grandparent's fire.

When the time had come for the BIWB to attend school, he'd been thrust into an environment inhabited in the main by Irish Catholics. Lincoln had been an area where traditionally, Irish families had settled and most of their kids had attended the school

99

known as SSPP. British schooling of the 1970's had come as a shock to the BIWB who, as a new boy yet again, had been treated unkindly by the other kids, who'd tried to bully the naive newcomer. Having experienced the kindness of the Carmelite monks back in Malta, he'd cynically sought out the school's resident priest and given him a hard luck story with a view to scrounging money from him. Ginger had worked his charm and Father "L" had indeed given him some cash! Not satisfied with his childish manipulation of the kind priest, the BIWB – still in street kid mode - had thanked him, saying that he could use the money for a haircut, but that there wouldn't be enough left over to buy food with! Having managed to extract more money from the clergyman, he'd gone off to spend it - not at the barber's shop, but on cigarettes and goodies! In fact, the boy had been given lunch money every day by social services, but rather than queue up to spend it on school dinners, he'd hung out with the cool kids instead. Back then "cool" had been to spend half of your lunch money on a small bag of fries and a bread roll with which to make a "chip butty." The remaining half of the social services money had been enough to buy a couple of single cigarettes from the newsagent – old habits and all that! Then, away from the "squares" back in the school playground, he'd smoke and joke with the rest of the gang.

In some lessons, such as that presided over by the music teacher, utter chaos had reigned with the kids literally running riot. Ginger had watched in amazement as his fellow pupils, unchecked by *Cettina*, had sworn at the teacher and even lit up cigarettes in the classroom! The boy had opted out of metalwork classes in favour of home economics (He'd cheekily, but correctly figured that there would be a larger ratio of girls to boys baking cakes than in the metalwork class) He'd once poked his head around the door of the latter, and instead of seeing pupils engrossed in clever technical projects, he'd seen a couple of them running around using oxy-acetylene torches to melt pennies into red-hot blobs of glowing copper! Academically, SSPP hadn't been exactly been a favourite of the school inspectors and when the mathematics lesson came along, the maths teacher had a solution for dumb kids such as the newly arrived BIWB. This solution not only benefitted the impatient maths teacher, but also suited his colleague who

100

taught physical education. The deal worked thus: The kids who were unable to grasp the intricacies of logarithms, could be removed from the equation – so to speak - and the PE teacher - who made fibre-glass canoes for the school - gained an unending source of labour in the form of the young maths dunces. Mr "G" would appear at the start of the dreaded maths lesson and remove the grateful boys from the mysterious world of calculations, depositing them in his canoe workshop at the other end of the school. There, they'd be put to work smearing sticky resin onto sections of prickly fibreglass sheeting before pressing them into the moulds that would eventually turn them into brightly coloured canoes for the school's trips away.

Not long after he'd arrived at the school, another pupil had called him a "cunt" It could never have been said that the BIWB hadn't been more than capable of delivering a master class in Maltese swearing, but he hadn't been familiar with that particular insult or English swearwords generally. And so, later, back at 77 Greetwell road, he'd wandered into the kitchen where his Gran had been standing at the sink, cigarette in mouth, peeling potatoes for the evening meal. He'd innocently asked: 'Grandma, what's *cunt* mean?' The old girl had simply uttered a nicotine-hoarse chuckle and gone on with peeling the potatoes! Later, when the BIWB had learned the meaning of the insult, he'd cornered the kid who'd sworn at him, grabbing hold of him before shoving him into a wall. Unfortunately for him, he may have learned his first English swear word, but he was yet to experience the loyalty of the Irish clan to their own kind. In the school washroom that afternoon, he'd been confronted by an older boy with a wild look in his eyes and a "Don't fuck with me" swagger. Grabbing a handful of the ginger kid's shirt, he'd pulled out a sheath knife and threatened that if he should ever mess with his friend again, he'd stab him! (The knife wielding boy and the new kid would later become firm friends)

To the BIWB, used to much warmer climes, the snow and northern fog seemed to last forever and by February, the novelty of a Britain in the full grip of winter had begun to wear off. By the spring of the following year, it seemed as though the welcome for the boys at Greetwell Road had also started to wear thin. In retrospect, his elderly grandfather – who hadn't exactly been a model father to the kid's mother, had found it difficult to have a surly teenager and his younger sibling around the house. The BIWB hadn't exactly helped matters when he'd been suspected (rightly) of pinching his great-grandfather's cigarettes! As had been usual when it came to their futures, the boys hadn't been in on the plan to pack them off into the care of social services, and by the end of spring, they'd had their bags packed and found themselves at an assessment centre called Haven House in Birchwood, on the outskirts of Lincoln.

Haven House, set in woodland and equipped with it's own school room for those problem kids who hadn't attended school - in some cases for years; had been a temporary home to children from around six years old to troubled adolescents from a variety of disastrous family situations. The idea had been, that after a few weeks – extending to months in some cases – the kids would either be farmed out to foster parents, or to more suitable and long-term children's homes within the county. The staff had ranged from strict, older patrician figures to middle of the road "firm but fair" social workers. There had also been younger, more laid back social workers with whom the kids had had that little bit more in common. As for the "inmates" they were a mixture of the products of broken homes, petty criminals and those unwanted and problematic children from Lincolnshire's single parent families. Generally, the staff had been well-trained professionals, but it had to be said, that some of them had been woefully inadequate. In one case, such inadequacy would soon manifest itself during a conversation between the newly arrived boy and a member of staff. Ever since the BIWB had arrived in Britain, he'd suffered from almost constant headaches - whether this had been due to a change of climate, his new diet or some other factor, nobody had been sure. The solution, dreamed up by senior staff members, had been to send the boy to a psychiatric hospital to be seen by a psychiatrist! Waiting to be seen, the boy had sat in an interminable corridor surrounded by the shuffling ebb and flow of the hospital's residents; it hadn't looked unlike a scene from Jack Nicholson's *One Flew Over The Cuckoo's Nest!* After a while, a psychiatrist had popped his head from around the door to a consulting room and ushered the boy in. Grinning broadly, the quack had bid him a:

"Good morning, good afternoon and a good evening" all thrown into a single greeting. Ginger had wondered if the lunatics had taken over the asylum! He'd been shown the stock variety of ink splotch cards from which to make sense before being invited to give his interpretation of the patterns. The shrink had then asked him for his life story thus far, scribbled some indecipherable notes - not unlike the ink splotches - before looking up at the bemused kid and asking him whether he'd like to be admitted to the hospital for a while. The boy's 'no thank you doctor' had replaced his initial unspoken reaction of: 'no fuckin' thanks mate!' and with some relief, he'd taken leave of the doctor and grim hospital before walking out to the car park where his social worker had been waiting.

Apart from the headaches - which had been so debilitating that the boy had literally banged his head against the wall, he'd also become withdrawn, preferring to keep his own council. One morning, while with some other kids in the recreation room, the boy, who'd been throwing darts at a dartboard on the wall, took it into his head to throw a dart at a girl who'd been minding her own business playing billiards. The boy had absolutely no idea what had compelled him to do this, but with the dart literally sticking in the poor girl's backside, she'd ran off screaming to alert the staff. It may have been the head banging that had prompted his carers to send him to see the shrink, or it may have been the fact that he had used the girl's behind as target practice; but it had been one of the more enlightened social workers who had taken him to one side, looked straight into his eyes and shouted: 'Just because "F" (the man) was a shit to you, it doesn't mean you can go around doing as you please and not speaking to anyone!' This good old-fashioned telling off had had the desired effect of shaking the boy out of his self-pity and from that day on, he'd begun to open up a bit more and to integrate with the other kids at the home. The boy had also taken on the weekly task of washing the deputy head's sports car, for which he'd earned fifty pence. With the money that he earned for car washing, weekly pocket money for doing chores around the house and a generous clothing allowance, the BIWB had come a long way from his trousers with side zippers, Doris shoes, Wellington boots - and stealing empty bottles for their deposit!

103

There'd been an older girl at Haven House ("J") – a gangling girl, who kind of shuffled around the place, and had the misfortune of having been born with eyes that had looked in different directions. "J" had been adorned with several homemade tattoos, and the boy; feeling rebellious, but giving no regard to the fact that the girl's vision had left a lot to be desired, had agreed to be tattooed by her. The process had involved securing a bottle of Indian ink, which was to be pooled on the area to be tattooed, scrounging a sewing needle from the staff under the pretence of practicing needlework on a handkerchief, and the ability of the artist's subject/victim, to withstand the pain of a blunt needle being jabbed repeatedly into the skin. The BIWB – having been caught up in the whole Bruce Lee thing – had elected to have the actor's name written permanently on his upper right arm. "J" had placed the boy's arm on a table before gripping it tightly to stretch and keep the skin taut. Pouring on the jet-black ink, her wonky eyes swiveling chameleon-like, she'd taken hold of the sewing needle and proceeded to stab – at varying depths – at the kid's arm. Even before the "B" had been completed, the boy had known that he'd not be able to withstand the pain of another seven letters, and halfway into the "R" he'd told the maniacal looking "J" to stop! In her gruff Linconlshire accent, she'd called him a "Babby" but nonetheless, had ceased stabbing his arm. The boy's plea for the cessation of torture by needle had probably been a smart move; particularly when, after swabbing away the blood and surplus ink he'd surveyed the results of "J's" handiwork. Despite there having only been one and a half letters on his throbbing arm, they hadn't been remotely straight with the unfinished "R" sloping down at quite an angle!

One afternoon, along with two or three other kids, the boy had "run away" from home to visit the house in Scunthorpe where one of the older ex-residents now lived with his father. The intention had been to get away from the home and stay with him for a while. The twenty-four miles to the steel-producing town affectionately known as "Sunny Scunny" had been a fair distance to travel for kids with neither money nor mode of transport, but they'd reached it later that evening by hitchhiking. They'd managed to find the older boy's house on a rundown estate and after knocking on the door they'd been greeted by the kid's father telling them in no uncertain terms that they should "Fuck off!" The runaway's plan hadn't extended to what they would do in such a situation and they'd wandered around the dark and dismal town, hungry and deflated. Eventually, they'd plucked up the courage to phone the staff at Haven House and had all piled into a phone booth from where they had made a reverse charge call to the home. As the demoralised kids had been crammed into the phone box, a police patrol had spotted them and quizzed them as to what they were doing wandering around town. Taking them back to the police station, the runaways had been put into cells with the instruction that should they need anything, they should press the buzzer. Of course this had been all part of their sick humour, and when the boy had duly pressed his buzzer to request some food, the bobbies - no doubt having a good chuckle over their "just press the buzzer gag," had simply ignored the ginger kid's attempt at attracting their attention! After what seemed like forever, the kids had been let out of their cells and taken back to Haven House by a social worker and upon arrival, the formidable Miss "B" had been on the front lawn to greet them. Arms folded over her ample bosom, she'd told the miscreants that there was no food for them and that they were to go straight to bed. When the kids had wearily climbed the stairs to bed, they'd discovered that Miss "B" had trashed their beds meaning that they'd had to remake them before clambering in with empty stomachs! More tough love…

Integration with the other kids at Haven House had included getting close to one of the girls and receiving a seductive invitation to visit her bedroom one night. The girl's and boy's rooms had been at opposite ends of the house and at night were further isolated by creaky fire doors at the end of the corridors. When the night came for him to sneak to "C's" room, the lustful ginger kid had waited for the night staff to turn in before creeping to the other side of the house, through the very creaky doors and along the corridor to "C's" bedroom. Once there, they'd wasted no time and the boy, having peeled off his social services issue pyjamas, had slipped into bed beside the already naked girl, who had seemed very experienced despite her age. Unlike his peers at the home, this had been the BIWB's first encounter of an amorous kind, and he'd fumbled about until he'd managed to manoeuvre his sweaty body into the required position. Once there, to the disgust of the tut-tutting girl, he'd kept still, expecting nature to take over! Sighing, the impatient "C" had informed him that he'd have to create some movement if he expected a "result!" Sneaking back to his own room, the boy had been blissfully unaware that "C" had already been claimed by one of the other boys. "M" was a stocky, verging-on-fat kid, who idolised Elvis Presley and styled himself accordingly - right down to delivering grating renditions of Presley's catalogue. The first the boy had known of "M's" claim on "C" had been when coming down the stairs one morning, "M" who had been hiding under the stairs, had ambushed him, punching him in the stomach and knocking the wind from his body!

There had been another girl at Haven House, a little bit older than the others and who dressed and acted like a grown woman. The boy had been besotted with "J" but hadn't dared act on his natural impulse once he'd learned that she had a suitor – an older boy of around eighteen. To the younger kids, he'd been the epitome of cool. With his *Vespa* scooter adorned mod-style with numerous mirrors and the foxtail hanging from the whiplash antenna, *Foxy* had cut quite a dash in all his gear. The "Mod" used to meet the younger kids down by the stream at the back of the house, sometimes handing out cigarettes and the girls loved him. The boy had once inadvertently seen "J" in her underwear and had blushed red as a beetroot! "J" had just smiled coyly and told him not to worry about it. Ginger and "C's" spurned lover had eventually become friends; this had been in part, due to the fact that "Elvis" – upon hearing gossip and rumour by the other kids to the effect that Ginger had begun to take karate lessons - had been anxious that the boy he'd sneakily ambushed in the stairwell, may have been about to seek reprisal for the punch in the stomach. Not fancying a fair and out in the open fight, he'd gone to great lengths to ingratiate himself. As for the BIWB - he'd never gone near the girl who'd taken his virginity again – not because he'd feared "M's" reprisals, but because of the girl's humiliating impatience with him in the bedroom!

Truth be known, it had actually been the boy's older brother who, back in London and swept along with Bruce Lee mania, had been taking martial arts lessons. Whenever he'd visited Ginger at the home, he'd taught him a couple of karate moves and even

106

given him a Charles Atlas book to learn from (Atlas had been the strongman of the day, a kind of Arnold Schwarzenegger type.) The book had been a "do it yourself" affair which had included diagrams of muscle building exercises which could be carried out at home using props readily available in everyday life such as chairs. One of the female social workers; an older lady with a good heart, had noticed the boy's enthusiasm for body building and taken him home to meet her husband. A keen body builder in his day, the lady's husband had taken the boy under his wing and made him a barbell fashioned from a broom handle and old tin cans filled with concrete. He'd also dug out a pair of rusty old chest expanders from his shed and schooled the boy in their use. Slowly but surely, exercise and a decent diet had gradually begun to put muscle on the bony frame, long since made skinny by the hungry days in Malta.

Just as he'd begun to settle in at Haven House, he'd been told that his assessment was at an end and he was to be moved to a new and more permanent children's home called Cherry Tree House on the notorious estate of Saint Giles, not far from Lincoln's city centre. Coincidentally, Saint Giles had been home to the knife wielding kid who he'd encountered after challenging the boy who'd called him a "cunt" at school. By this time though, they'd become friends, and just being friends with the kid and his blade - who had a big family on the estate - had guaranteed Ginger safe passage through some of the more lawless parts of the immediate area. In fact, he'd become so close to *knife kid,* that he had taken to visiting him at his house where, one afternoon, to mark the occasion of the arrival of the 1970's fashion of male earrings reaching Saint Giles, they'd agreed to pierce each other's left ears. (A right ear piercing was for homosexuals only apparently!) The pain of the Haven House homemade tattoo consigned to distant memory, he'd more than happily agreed to indulge in some more amateur body mutilation. They'd chosen the Irish kid's back doorstep for the location from which to carry out the mutual operation. Placing ice-cubes on either side of Ginger's ear lobe – by way of anesthetic, and "sterilising" a large darning needle in the flame of a cigarette lighter, *knife kid* had forced it painfully through the boy's ear lobe, performing a crude and crooked, but effective piercing! When it had been Ginger's turn to reciprocate the procedure, he'd felt so sick, that he'd almost fainted! Telling the disgusted boy that he felt ill, he'd cried off darning needle duty. *Knife kid* had called him a big baby, shrugged his shoulders and going into the house in search of a mirror, he'd gone ahead and pierced his own ear! Needless to say, within a few days of getting his ear run through with a darning needle, the boy's ear lobe had become infected and it had been a few weeks before he'd been able to insert the plain but fashionable, hooped "sleeper" that back then, had been all the rage.

Cherry Tree, formed part of a trio of children's homes, set out literally in a triangle, with the other houses named: Spring House, and The Homestead. He'd actually enjoyed his time at Cherry Tree where the atmosphere had been more relaxed and with a feeling of permanency. Haven House had encouraged the kids to address the staff as Mr., Mrs. or Miss. By comparison, his new home was run along more family-type lines and the staff members there were referred to as: "auntie" or "uncle" with even the cleaning ladies expecting to be called by their Christian names. The kids at Cherry Tree were by and large, settled and long term residents, but there had still been an element of what social services called "damaged children" and a couple of the older kids had chequered past lives. Nonetheless, the BIWB had fitted in among the various personalities and spent the rest of that long hot summer in good company. Back then; evening and weekend entertainment had consisted of playing 45's on a *Dansette* record player in the laundry room, where the kids had been allowed to make as much noise as they'd liked. There among the laundry, they'd listened to the hits of the day such as *Abba, The Sweet, Slade, Mud* and even Johnny Cash! By this time, approaching sixteen years old, he'd had less than a year of schooling left, and still at SSPP, the prospects of gaining any meaningful qualifications were minimal to say the least – certainly where mathematics had been concerned!

Not long after settling into Cherry tree House, the boy had started attending martial arts classes at the Yarborough Sports Centre, which had been a twenty-minute walk through the bandit country that had been Saint Giles. Still inspired by the Bruce Lee phenomenon, he'd originally sought out Kung Fu lessons, but had only been able to find a bespectacled teacher of Aikido. Dressed in his skirt-like kit, the teacher had performed graceful wheeling throws with seemingly effortless aplomb while emphasising the flexibility his students must achieve. To that end, he'd had his young students performing push-ups on their bent over wrists! Impatient with his lack of progress in what required years of practice to even master the basics, he'd eventually stumbled upon Phil and Ray – two gritty instructors who twice a week, traveled the not inconsiderable distance from Sheffield in South Yorkshire, to Lincoln. They taught Shukokai karate in the same sports centre as the Aikido lessons and the BIWB, having watched a lesson, enrolled in their class. Given money by social services with which to buy kit, the boy had decided to go for a black karate suit instead of the traditional white; this had only made him stand out when making a mistake, and Phil would normally shout:'Oi! Black cat! What the fuck do you think you're doing?' He'd then make the boy in the ostentatious black suit do push-ups on his knuckles while repeating the mantra of: 'Karate men feel no pain, except when paying subs!'

Chapter Eight
Shedding The Wellington Boots
'Put it in a bucket'

Predictably, when the time had drawn near for his final school exams, the boy had been given the same non-existent encouragement he'd received during his maths/canoe making lessons; he'd not been remotely encouraged to study for, let alone take his exams. The choices of going on to sixth form or college had been neither explained nor offered to him. In the event, he'd taken English and art with the latter being graded more on photography than his talent at drawing. He'd passed both with a lowly "C" grade and left school in 1977 at the age of sixteen. At the invitation of his older brother, who'd still been looking out for him, he'd moved into his maisonette on Albert Square in the borough of Newham, London. Thirty-five years later, Newham would be host to the London 2012 Olympics, but you would never had guessed that this could happen back in those strike-ridden days of 1977. Ginger, freed from the shackles of school, social services and authority, now stumbled innocently into a harsh world of high unemployment and the reality of a country spiraling into debt. As is usual in a recession, decent jobs are hard to come by, especially for a sixteen-year-old kid with no more than English and art CSE's to his name. Menial work, however, is always available to those willing to work – after all: it's the same today with hard working Eastern European immigrants willing to shoulder the grinding burden of manual labour that those comfortable on benefit handouts shun. In London, back in 1977, the same had been the case, except the immigrants back then had consisted mainly of first generation Poles, Irishmen, Afro-Caribbeans and North Africans. The boy had worked alongside all them in the city bakery, where his brother had found him employment.

Superslice Bakeries baked bread from several London premises at that time: Liverpool Street, where the boy's brother worked the night shift, Edmonton in North London and Old Street on the Islington/City of London border, and it had been there that the boy had been put to work on the day shift. His shift had started at six in the morning - which had come as a bit of a shock to the boy. In fact most days, he'd failed to make it on time, having real issues with getting out of bed (no Maltsese man threatening to tip water over him!). More than once, his brother had arrived back home from his night shift, to find Ginger still in bed when he should have been long gone! He'd invested in a giant wind-up alarm clock, but even this had failed to do the trick. Ernie, the Polish foreman in charge of the early shift at *Superslice,* had been patient with the new kid and offered advice on how to get his backside out of bed. Ernie's suggestions had included putting his alarm clock into a bucket to amplify the sound, and/or, placing the clock above his head, and wrapping a piece of string around the alarm winder key. The theory behind this idea had been, that as the alarm went off and the winder unwound, it would lower the string onto the boy's face, tickle him and wake him up! The boy did try these bizarre methods, but in the case of the bucket, it just had the effect of muffling the sound of the bells, and as for the winder, it merely let the string down a foot or so before becoming tangled, wrapping itself around the key and climbing back up and away from its intended target of the slumbering boy's face!

When he had managed to get up in time, he'd yet again borrowed his brother's wheels – this time a trendy *Chopper* bicycle, and ridden the few miles to Old street. Once there, he'd spend the day as general dogsbody, carrying out such tasks as feeding *Manitoba* flour from heavy sacks into the giant hopper that fed the giant bread-mixing bowls below, and sweeping the vast bakery floor. Back then, smoking had been allowed even on the premises of a bakery, and although there had been a designated smoking area, this had been inside the building, not far from the food preparation area. As the boy had swept the floor, his brush had picked up the odd cigarette end among the spilled flour and when the foreman had seen him about to throw the contents of his dustpan away, he'd stopped him, instructing him instead to sieve the contents of his dustpan and utilise the grey coloured ash and flour mixture to dust down the bread rolls waiting to go into the oven! This practice had probably been one of the reasons why the boy had never resorted to taking *Superslice* bread home with him! Occasionally the boy had helped out with rolling pieces of dough into the first stages of bread rolls known as *Abercorn,* but he job he'd liked most of all, had been that of slashing the dough with a razor-like tool just before the trays of rolls were loaded into the oven. The slashes were intended to give the dough an outlet from which steam could escape and so prevent the rolls from bursting while being baked, and had harked back to his cactus slashing days. He'd been one of the youngest employees at Old Street and had shared the dough-working tables with the likes of the Algerian, who idolised the Labour MP Tony Benn, and the big Londoner who constantly bemoaned the state of the economy and offered comment on the scandals of the day such as: those "nasty" *Sex Pistols,* and how the members of *Abba* had split with their respective husbands and wives to be with each other - disgraceful in his opinion. Then there had been the unintelligible giant of an Afro-Caribbean man who, dressed in denim dungarees, spent the day playing with himself while muttering unintelligibly with the odd maniacal laugh thrown in.

When he'd gone upstairs to the very basic canteen for his thirty-minute break, he'd hardly found a place to sit - filled as it had been, with snoring men sprawled out and getting some much needed sleep. These men had been known as "jobbers", men who for fourteen pounds cash in hand, had already worked a nightshift wherever there had been a shortfall in labour - either at Old Street, Liverpool Street or Edmonton. After their night of "jobbing" the men would go straight to work at their normal place of work where they would sleep walk their way through the day. He'd never really understood why some of the guys had worn sunglasses while working inside the bakery, but imagined it was to prevent them being seen with their eyes closed as they slept on their feet! The boy had accepted the offer of jobbing at another bakery one night and had spent the shift surrounded by heavily accented Irishmen jabbering away in what to the boy, had been a foreign language. Shattered, he'd gone home for an hour's rest before his normal day shift, and not daring to close his eyes, he'd stretched out on the old settee to relax before going in for his day shift. It had been in that trance-like state that he'd heard the Capital Radio announcer telling London that, Elvis Presley had died. He'd never forget that day; not because he'd been a big fan of the "King" but because in his semi-conscious state, it had seemed surreal and all the more momentous as the newsreader's disembodied voice percolated into his sleep deprived mind. Actually, Elvis or no

Elvis; staying up all night had provided one of the rare occasions when he'd actually made it to work on time without the aid of buckets or string!

The converted maisonette on Albert Square, home to the boy and his older brother had comprised one bedroom, (in what must at one time have been the sitting room), a dining room, cellar, and a tiny kitchen without a cooker. The boy had shared the bedroom with his brother but on occasion also slept in the dining room. There hadn't been a bathroom and they'd have to wash in the kitchen sink where there hadn't been any hot water. Cooking and heating water for washing, had been provided by a *Primus* stove – one of those portable camping-type affairs which ran on methylated spirit and had to be kept constantly primed by pumping a small plunger to keep the pressure up and the blue flame roaring. With no bath or shower facilities, the boys had built a kind of lean-to affair in the back garden with the sides and sloping roof being constructed from sheets of corrugated plastic nailed to a wooden frame. A metal tank had been filled and then heated using the trusty, hissing *Primus.* A length of garden hose, fitted with the sprinkler end of a watering can or some such item, had been attached to the tank and gravity had done the rest! Talk about necessity being the mother of invention!

One Saturday, while listening to Kenny Everett's *Captain Kremmen* on Capital Radio, the boy's brother had announced that the daughter of the African family next door had decided to run away from home. The boy had known of the friendship between the girl and his brother, which had been purely platonic, and probably forged through an understanding of excessively strict parenting. When the boy's brother had told him of the girl's intentions, he hadn't realised that the place to which she'd chosen to run away to, had been non other than next door – their place! She'd somehow managed to smuggle herself in, and within a couple of days, her father - a fierce looking man with crude tribal scars etched into his face, had begun to suspect that his errant daughter, in her bid for freedom, had only got as far as next door. When the boys had refused to answer the door to him, the big African had begun to hassle the boys whenever they'd stepped outside. An audacious plan - intended to put him off the scent, had been hatched. The idea; brainchild of Ginger's older brother, had involved going to the local police station and complaining about their neighbour's harassment of them. First though, the girl had to be hidden, which she duly was – in the cellar among the junk, from where the boy's brother had taken the precaution of removing the light bulb. At the police station, a constable had agreed to accompany the boys back to their house and carry out a search to establish that the girl wasn't there. Ginger, far less confident in the venture than his older sibling, had watched in horror as the officer had opened the door to the cellar: surely the cop would easily find the girl and they'd be in the sticky and brown stuff! Plod flicked the light switch, a couple of times before he'd been brazenly told that due to an electrical fault, the light didn't work. To the boy's amazement, the cop had taken their word for it and not even descended the first few steps to the girl's hiding place! Going back outside, he'd gone next door to have a word with the girl's father warning him to stop harassing the boys! The next day, realising that he couldn't keep her hidden forever, the girl's co-conspirator had spoken to her and she'd agreed to return home to face the music. The only question had been, how they would be able to achieve this without being seen by her suspicious father. The solution they'd agreed on, had been for her to be dressed in Ginger's clothes, with his scarf wrapped around her face and wearing the boy's crash helmet with the visor down. Boldly stepping out into the street with the girl, disguised as his brother, he'd sat her on the back of his motorbike and ridden off. A few streets away, she'd dismounted, changed back into her own clothes and walked the couple of blocks back to her house as if she'd just returned from her mysterious sojourn!

Not long after the "girl in the basement" adventure, the boy, now with a secure job, had become eligible to take out loans and finance. Seeing a shiny green new *Honda* SS50 moped in the showroom, he'd wanted to emulate his brother's motorcycling, and to the delight of the salesman, down on his commission in those days of depression, Ginger had stepped unbidden, right into his office. Swayed by the swanky fairing, racing trim, and complimentary nylon sports jacket, the boy had eagerly signed a three-year hire purchase agreement and left the showroom with his prize. With the 1977 registration plate of RME756R, the little

frog-green Honda had been described in the brochure as something
like this:

*The SS50 (Super Sports) with a power output of 2.5 BHP can
reach a top speed of 49MPH! A delight to behold, with its long
slim race style tank, short racing seat, telescopic forks, a gorgeous
Hi-Line exhaust with heat shield and a superb range of new
'Candy' metallic paint finishes. This all adds up to make it the best
looking 50ccc sports bike on the market, and with an overhead
camshaft engine, the only four stroke as well!*

Back then; the only requirement to ride a moped had been to be
sixteen-years old, be the holder of a provisional driving licence,
and to display "L" plates on the bike. No "Compulsory Basic Test"
had been needed in 1977 and with absolutely no instruction on
how to ride the thing, the newest addition to the chaotic London
roads - having traded in his speedy Doris Shoes for some hot
wheels - sped off down the road behind his brother on the bigger
Suzuki. Half a mile down the road, disaster had struck, and
panicking at the sudden appearance of a delivery van, he'd
grabbed a handful of front brake lever, locked up the front wheel
and collided with the side of the van! His brother had placated the
irate van driver and the boy, his exuberance tamed, had ridden the
sorry-looking *Honda* the rest of the way to Albert Square with the
sporty fairing cracked, a bent pedal and one of the indicator stalks
dangling forlornly from its frame!

Not content with emulating his brother's motorcycling, Ginger
had decided one day to look like him too. Purchasing some cheap
DIY hair dye in jet black from the local supermarket, he'd rushed
home to apply it. Pumping up the faithful *Primus* stove, he'd
heated up some water, and bending over the kitchen sink, had
massaged the gooey dye into his hair. He'd just finished when his
bemused brother had remarked that he'd need to dye his ginger
eyebrows while he was at it. Realising his mistake, the boy had
simply scooped the remaining dye from the bottom of the sink
with his hands and smeared it over his eyebrows. Never one to
read instructions, the boy's impulsive behaviour had resulted in
creating a caricature of Groucho Marx! Luckily for him, it had
been summer, and for the next six weeks, he'd had to resort to
wearing huge sunglasses to cover his massive black "eyebrows"

After less than a year of failing to get up for his early morning shift, the terrible bathroom arrangements and general boredom, the boy had decided to jack it in and return to Lincoln. Taking the battered moped with him and without even the kernel of a plan, he'd traveled back to the only place familiar to him in the country. He'd gone to visit Cherry Tree House, where Mrs. "N" who'd had a soft spot for him, had arranged a job interview for the position of grill chef. This had been with the now defunct Berni Inns steakhouses. A social worker had been kind enough to accompany him to the interview, and had put a word in with the manager – Mr. "D" who was a dour Scot with a mischievous glint in his eye. Securing the position, he'd been issued with starched chef's whites, a red neckerchief and a proper tall chef's hat. Starting under the tutelage of one of the assistant managers, he'd been instructed in the fine art of cooking steaks, gammon, plaice in batter and the preparation of salads and prawn cocktails. The assistant manager - "C" – a sweaty overweight man, who preyed on any waitress unfortunate enough to find herself cornered in the cellar by him, had passed the boy fit for work as a grill chef and a new career at Berni Inns (The Falcon, Saltergate, Lincoln) had begun. He'd been taught how to cook steaks ranging from "blue" to "very well done" and how to ensure that an order for a variety of dishes for the same table could be prepared and served simultaneously. He'd been shown how to make decent and non-lumpy batter for the plaice, instructed in the art of preparing Dover sole and schooled in the emergency procedure for what to do if one ran out of defrosted plaice: Nip to another restaurant and borrow some maybe? No, get a frozen block from the freezer, fill a sink with boiling water and plunge the solid and unyielding block into the sink until it surrendered and could be pulled apart! Older, leftover steaks, which had begun to turn green and smell, were to be washed in vinegar and served up! Between the almost rotten meat and hastily defrosted plaice, it was a wonder that the customers hadn't contract salmonella! The boy had also learned to tell a good steak from a bad one just by looking at it and at times, this had suited his rebellious young nature. The restaurant layout at Berni's had been designed with the kitchen completely visible to the public with the intention of allowing the diners to watch the chef at work; this had worked both ways though, and the chef was able to see who his customers were and who was ordering what. Accordingly, the good steaks would be served to the pleasant customers – who sometimes bought him a drink - and the bad ones, tough as old boots, were reserved for those surly customers who were fond of sending their meals back to the kitchen with complaints!

With a regular wage coming in, the boy had been able to rent a bedsitting room in a three-storey house on Yarborough Road, belonging to a curious regular at The Falcon. Gangling and delightfully eccentric, the man had long dark curly hair in the style of Louis the 13th and wore a beard that wouldn't have disgraced Sir Walter Raleigh; his appearance had reminded the boy of a lion. One of the two other inhabitants in the Edwardian house on Yarborough Road, had been a timid and neurotic Welsh woman – who as far as the boy could tell was the lion man's lover and who, on occasion - when Lion Man had been out - had scuttled up to the boy's attic room and confided in him about her apparently problematic relationship with his landlord. The second tenant had been an intense mustachioed man in his early thirties who habitually dressed as a *Teddy Boy.* The man had, it seemed, been an ex-soldier, who from what the boy could glean, had become mentally disturbed after a tour of Northern Ireland. Ginger had never really discovered what traumatic experiences the guy had been through, but had been astonished when one day, Teddy Boy had invited him into his room, whereupon opening a wardrobe, he'd extracted a cloth, which when unwrapped, had revealed a Browning 9mm semi-automatic pistol, of the type used by the British army at the time. Not offering an explanation as to how he'd come to be in possession of such a lethal weapon (most probably he'd picked it up during a house search in Northern Ireland and kept it), Teddy Boy had thoughtfully stroked his luxuriant moustache, re-wrapped the pistol and replaced it in his wardrobe before sternly warning the boy that he was never to tell anyone else about it. The deranged ex-soldier had terrified Ginger, who'd never established what Teddy Boy did for a living, but assumed that he did nothing; given that he seemed to spend most days sitting in the public gallery of Lincoln Crown Court observing proceedings. He'd sometimes accompanied Teddy Boy when he went out into the surrounding fields with his legally held air rifles and he'd let the boy use one of them to shoot pigeons. He'd appeared paranoid though, and if ever they had crossed paths with other people walking through the field, he'd inexplicably hiss that the boy should point his rifle at the ground and shoot into the mud. The house on Yarborough Road had certainly been inhabited by some odd people!

After returning to Lincoln, the boy had maintained contact with the "aunties" and "uncles" at Cherry Tree and as a result, had begun to see a girl of his own age who lived next door at Spring House. He'd been invited to spend New Year's Eve at the home and it had been arranged that he stay the night. Spring House, had been the work place of "Aunty" "C" who had been known to be more than a little flirtatious; particularly with the soldiers from 50 Missile Regiment Royal Artillery, whose recruiting area had been Lincolnshire and Humberside. Once a year they'd visited the town on KAPE tour (Keeping the Army in the Public Eye). The soldiers had toured the county with the intention of drumming up interest in the army; but in particular, their regiment, that at the time, had been based in Menden, Germany. The camouflage-clad gunners had set up mobile shooting ranges and trampolines, and brought along exciting equipment such as *Honest John* missile launchers (a nuclear capable rocket system), with which to tempt the listless teenagers from the surrounding area. The children's homes with their captive audience of adolescents, keen to escape the drudgery of 1970's Lincoln, had been ripe for the recruiter's picking, and so a couple of days had usually been put aside for the soldiers to display their wares in Saint Giles, where they would and try to lure those kids (without a criminal record) into an exciting career - filled ostensibly - with skiing and snorkeling in far off exotic countries. The insatiable meat grinder that had been Northern Ireland hadn't featured in any of the army's glossy recruiting brochures, and the kids had been captivated by the tanned and fit mustachioed men in camouflage – as had Aunty "C" who had been more than a little welcoming!

On New Year's Eve, the boy had gone to Spring House, arriving for the evening party. He'd been met at the door by the voracious Aunty "C", who'd announced that she would take him to see the room in which he was to sleep after the party. Leaving his girlfriend in the lounge, he'd followed the woman upstairs.

Opening the door to a bedroom, she'd ushered him inside, closed the door and thrown herself onto the bed while pulling the boy on top of her and French kissing him! Immediately and callously forgetting the innocent girl downstairs, he'd responded. Since his disastrous experience with the girl from Haven House, he'd only got to grips with one other girl and she'd been patiently waiting for him in the lounge downstairs! Pulling the more than a little aroused boy off her, Aunty "C" had whispered that if he wanted more of the same, he should come to her bedroom later that night – which, without even thinking, he'd done. Despite exerting a great deal more energy than he had while labouring over the girl with the same initial, back in the hot summer of 1976, he'd nonetheless failed to satisfy the "aunty" with the penchant for soldiers – and quite frankly – anything remotely male!

Back at *The Falcon* on Lincoln's Saltergate, the boy had slowly begun to become a valued member of the catering team. He'd flourished and despite the petulance of youth, had embraced the art of grilling steaks. Working unaided, he'd happily pushed out orders for up to 120 meals a night, although, on the busier weekend nights, he'd accepted the help of a chip-frying assistant. The assistants had come in the form of such characters as the Afghan coat-wearing trainee teacher; a hippie who grew his own cannabis, and an eccentric middle-aged woman "A" who described her place of abode as the "Mouse House" and who in the midst of an extremely busy night, had the habit of gazing earnestly into the boy's eyes and saying things like 'Shall I put the chippy-wippies in yet?' to which he'd think – but not say – 'Yes "A" for fuck sake, put the fuckin' chips in!' One morning, the Afghan coat-clad trainee teacher, had rushed up to the boy, and in full cannabis-induced paranoia mode hissed: 'The drug squad are watching me - here, take this!' Thrusting a carrier bag filed with very weak homegrown cannabis into the boy's hands, he'd fled while looking theatrically over his shoulder!

Then there'd been the boy's fellow chef - "G" - who'd worked in the restaurant downstairs. "G" had been experimenting with drug taking when he'd worked at *The Falcon* and the boy had, to a certain extent, been drawn in. Cannabis resin had been all the rage back then and agreeing to accompany "G" back to his seedy bedsitting room between shifts, the boy had followed "G's" lead as he'd stuck a lump of resin onto a pin before lighting it and placing it under a glass. Once the glass had filled with smoke, they'd inhaled the resultant smoke and giggled the time away until the evening shift, when, limbs numb from cannabis smoking, they'd thrown steaks onto the grill with gay abandon! Stoned or not, that night the boy had cooked up a storm for the cast of the then popular soap opera *Crossroads* who had been performing at the local theatre. So pleased had they been with the boy's against all odds cannabis- influenced efforts, they'd bought him a drink! The boy's drug experimentation had ended on the day "G" had given him a blue-coloured tablet, which he'd swallowed just before his night shift. Heaven knows what it had contained, but he'd spent the evening pacing up and down, feeling trapped, full of paranoia and wishing the shift away! "G" had later fallen out of favour with the management, after arriving at *Berni's* one day with some stickers depicting a cartoon image of a chef bearing the slogan: "I'm a little chef" "G" and the boy had thought the stickers quite cool; so much so, that they'd stuck them onto their chef's hats. They'd been blissfully unaware that they were advertising Berni's rival, *The Little Chef,* until the manager had spotted the idiots scoring one for the rival team and told them to: 'Get those fuckin stickers off your hats, you half-wits!'

When they'd not been working, the boy and "G" had enjoyed visiting Berni's Cellar Bar. Located, as the name suggests - in the basement. The bar had been run by "D" - a self-styled manager of local up and coming pop groups. With his bouffant blonde hair, stiffened with hair lacquer and red trousers so tight they left nothing to the imagination, he'd pranced about the place with a briefcase giving off the air of someone just passing through – waiting for his big break. Dark, dingy and atmospheric, the Cellar Bar had been a million miles away from the plush restaurant on the top floor and made even the bar on the ground floor, seem highbrow in comparison. Equipped with a loud jukebox pumping out such classics as *America's "Horse With No Name"* and *"Follow You Follow Me"* by *Genesis*, the bar had attracted hordes of cannabis-befuddled hippies in their floor-length Afghan coats. Occasionally local rednecks would gatecrash and real Wild West saloon-type brawls would kick off – chairs smashed over hippie's backs, flying glasses, pool cues turned into weapons – the whole nine yards!

The boy's life education had blossomed at *Berni's,* and on the occasion of his seventeenth birthday, he'd been given a birthday card by the barmaids who worked the *Stonebow* Bar on the ground floor. A poor relation to the first floor restaurant where the boy cooked steaks, the *Stonebow* had taken its name from the iconic stone arch on Lincoln's High street. The south gate to the city, it was built in the 15th century on the site of the original Roman gate. The *Stonebow* Bar catered to the lunchtime customers who had been more interested in a bar snack and a pint of Lager than their evening counterparts upstairs who in contrast, spent the evening munching their way through prawn cocktails, fillet steak and the sophisticated cheeseboard of the day. Quaffing their after-dinner liquor coffees, they'd been oblivious to the flotsam and jetsam that had ebbed and flowed from the *Stonebow* Bar.

Opening his card and reading the good wishes from the downstairs bar staff, the boy had been about to return to his hot-plate upstairs, when one of the barmaids – "G" had taken him to one side and next to the stack of dirty glasses by the dishwasher, she'd offered him a birthday kiss! "G" had been a good ten years older than the boy and despite her buxom appearance; her heady perfume had lured him into her eager arms. He'd tentatively kissed her only to be enveloped in her ample arms. Crushing him to her huge breasts, "G" had meant business – this, the boy mused, had been one hell of a lot more than a birthday kiss, and there among the pile of beer glasses, he'd felt compelled to return her ardour! Finally releasing the boy from her suffocating embrace, she'd handed him a note that once he'd reached the safety of his kitchen, he'd read. In beautiful copperplate writing, the note, mimicking the script on an English banknote had read: "*I promise to pay the bearer on demand, the price of one good night.*" On the reverse, "G" (a married woman it should be said) had written her address and the date and time that, should he accept, would be suitable for him to cash in his promissory note! He had of course done what any hot blooded seventeen-year old would have done in his place, and when "G's" suggested day had had arrived, he'd been round her house like a rat up a drainpipe! According to the lustful barmaid, her husband worked nights and arriving at around eight

121

pm, the boy had been subjected to a sexual frenzy the likes of which his parish priest back in Ta'Lourdes would have sentenced him to an eternity of Hail Marys! He'd been a bit perturbed when a few days later, "G" had introduced him to her husband who'd arrived at the *Stonebow* to collect her after work. Although he'd never met the husband before, the man had been very familiar in his manner of talking to the boy and had even smarmily addressed him by his name. The young lothario had later wondered whether on the night when "G" had had her wicked way with him, her husband had actually been hiding in the wardrobe getting his kicks from his wife being serviced by the young chef!

One of the boy's most influential mentors back in the heady days of *Berni's* had been "R" - an ex-soldier turned assistant restaurant manager. A previous member of Lincolnshire's 50 Missile Regiment, he had at some point, been part of the KAPE tour which had set up shop outside the children's homes on Saint Giles – whether he'd had carnal knowledge of Aunty "C" the boy had never established! Tall, dark, worldly and always smartly dressed, "R" had been a strong influence on the young chef and he'd filled the boy's head with tales of his army days in Germany; the state- run brothels, endless supplies of beer, skiing trips and general camaraderie. "R" had introduced the boy to alcohol, and man, could he drink! Attempting – and failing miserably to keep up with "R's" seemingly Olympic capability for drinking Lager, his eager apprentice had been caught on several occasions surreptitiously ditching his beer into plant pots! "R's" motto had been that: bar snacks were for drunks and that it simply just wasn't cool to take one's jacket off. As a result - in contrast to the cool as a cucumber "R" - he'd spent hours drinking without first lining his stomach, and sweated buckets beneath his velvet jacket (very trendy back in the *Saturday Night Fever* 1970's!) at the disco bars! Failing miserably to match "R's" alcohol intake, he'd spent many an afternoon between shifts at *Berni's* literally crawling on his hands and knees to the nearest toilet in which to throw up! "R" had eventually moved on to manage another branch of *Berni's* and the fledgling chef, now a fairly accomplished drinker had begun to find his own way, influenced by the "cool" that had been his mentor.

As the boy's perceived ability to withstand pressure in the kitchen had developed, he'd been given the task of preparing the staff meals prior to the restaurant opening. Along with preparing roast chickens, defrosting fish, scrubbing and heating grill plates, cooking peas and boiling soup for the lunchtime session, he'd been expected to turn out staff meals. Admittedly, these had been pre-prepared and what one today would call "ready meals", but for an eighteen year old with the typical anger management issues of a teenager, it had at times proved to be too high a workload. He'd normally take it out on his surroundings - slamming the fridge door, swearing and generally huffing and puffing. One fateful day, he'd arrived late for work, and in a seemingly nightmarish world of flour, batter, greasy pre-cooked chickens and frozen blocks of plaice, he'd taken his eye off the ball and allowed the cauldron of tomato soup - hitherto simmering on the stove in readiness for the lunchtime menu – to boil over. In a fit of pique, he'd said something along the lines of: 'Fuck the lot of you' and walked out, leaving the restaurant without lunchtime chef! He'd wandered around for a while before, acting on impulse – his head still full of "R's" army tales – he'd walked into the Royal Marines recruiting office almost opposite *Berni's*.

The marine recruiting sergeant had looked the boy up and down before inviting him to sit down and take the entrance test. Once the paper had been placed before him, he's scanned through it with the incredulity of one who'd assumed that to join the marines would just be a matter of turning up and signing something. With the questions staring back at him, he'd begun to realise the drawbacks of having gone off to make canoes instead of learning mathematics! He'd not had an inkling how to work out long division and as for fractions; they'd been as much a mystery to him on that day in the Royal Marines office, as they'd been a couple of years previously at SSPP! Turning the page, he'd been confronted with semi-technical drawings depicting cogs, with the invitation to work out which cog turned another cog and why! He'd been OK with the English language section, but with everything else just staring back at him from the page, he'd gone for the scattergun approach; ticking random answers in the hope that some of them would be correct! Crestfallen, he'd handed in his paper at the end of his allotted time and after a brief wait, had been dismissed as "not very hot academically" and "not enthusiastic enough" Walking disconsolately out of the office, he'd wondered whether he should have at least solved the lack of enthusiasm bit by crashing through the door screaming: 'I WANNA BE A MARINE!'

Trudging unhappily back up the hill to the Lion Man's place, the rejected ex-grill chef had gone up to his room and had a good hard think. The following morning, painfully aware that in order to qualify for unemployment benefit, he'd have to have been made jobless – as oppose to *making himself* jobless – he'd resolved to go and see the manager at *The Falcon* and eat humble pie. Walking into Mr. "D's" office, he'd faced the humiliation of the supercilious stares from the secretary and other office staff before mercifully, Mr. "D" had taken him out of the office and the earshot of eavesdroppers. Sternly the Scotsman, twinkle missing from his eyes had asked the boy to give him one good reason why he should take him back. Looking down at the floor as forlornly as he could, he'd muttered how sorry he was and if given another chance it wouldn't happen again etc... Mr. "D" had kindly given the boy a chance, though truth be known, it would have been hard to find a replacement at such short notice and the assistant managers; who'd filled in during the boy's absence, had also made representations on the boy's behalf so as to get *them* the hell out of the kitchen!

And so life had gone on at *The Falcon* much as it had before the soup incident and the boy, growing in sexual confidence, had invited a barmaid from the *Stonebow* Bar, ("J") - a less than shy girl - to the cinema, where they'd watched a horror film. A few post-film drinks later, he'd taken her up to his attic room at the Lion Man's place, where after a bit of fumbling, he'd embarked upon his first experience of oral sex - and a disastrous first experience it had proved to be! As he'd submerged himself beneath the duvet and moved ever closer to the prize, his nostrils had been assailed by the unmistakable odour emanating from what could only have been described aesthetically as a badly wrapped kebab! As for the smell: it appeared that "J's" attention to personal hygiene had been lacking to say the least! Beating a tactical retreat, he'd started to work his way back up the girl's body in search of fresh air but "J" was having none of it and pushing the boy's head back whence it had come, she'd forced his face into confrontation with her unruly tangle of pubic hair! Resisting her efforts as gallantly as he possibly could under the circumstances, he'd broken free of her amorous grasp and resurfaced. Sighing a 'For fuck's sake' "J" had muttered something about "finishing it off herself" and had proceeded to do just that – with her fingers, not her tongue – it should be added! Meanwhile, somewhere downstairs, Teddy Boy was in his room oiling and polishing his illicit Browning 9mm pistol and Welsh Woman was sitting fretfully on her bed awaiting the Lion Man's return from *The Falcon* where he'd be lingering thoughtfully over his customary half pint of bitter.

Maintaining his links with Cherry Tree House like a kind of comfort blanket, the boy had visited the home a couple of times a month (and not to see Aunty "C" either!) Still riding his trusty *Honda* – tax, insurance and roadworthiness test - long since out of date – as was his driving licence – he'd zoomed over there one afternoon, parked it up outside and gone inside to say "Hello" He'd seen the cop car outside but thought nothing of it. Cherry Tree, had long since been what the local cops had referred to as a "tea stop" in other words, a place to take time out from their beat, put their feet up, chat up the female staff and drink tea. During the time that the boy had lived there, he'd got to know the most regular of the visiting cops, and finding them friendly and not too authoritarian; he'd got on well with them. On the afternoon of his latest visit, the boys in blue had greeted him warmly and he'd gone into the sitting room to catch up with the residents who he remembered from his own time there. Catch up complete; he'd had a cup of tea and some cake with the staff before jumping back onto his trusty moped and speeding off into the evening. Unbeknown to him, while the boy had been socialising, the "friendly" cops – obviously short on their motoring offences quota for the month – had pored all over the ginger kid's *Honda*. The first thing that they'd triumphantly noticed had been the tax disc – woefully out of date and almost obscured by the rust on it's holder; then when further checks had revealed the bike's lack of annual test certificate, the cops must have thought they'd struck the mother lode! Sitting in their patrol car outside Cherry Tree, the officers had watched the boy ride off, let him get a short distance away from the home and then innocently; as if they'd only just encountered him, they'd pulled him over. They had gone through the motions of asking him questions to which they already had answers and some to which they didn't, such as 'Did he have insurance? Did he have a driving licence?' Contritely answering that no, he didn't have insurance and yes, his licence had expired, he'd stood at the roadside while the cops had filled out reams of important-looking paperwork. Once Lincoln's finest had wrung every ounce of motoring offence out of the boy, they'd bid him good evening and instructed him to push the *Honda* the rest of the way home. Ginger though, in a display of rebellion – and feeling quite rightly that he'd had nothing more to lose, had waited until the cops had been out of sight before jumping back on and roaring off in to the night!

Not long after his brush with the law, Ginger had been offered the use of a much bigger bike – 500cc bigger in fact! The *Yamaha* XS550, a four-cylinder beast capable of speeds in excess of 120MPH, had been a restoration project and belonged to someone he'd known. You couldn't ride such a machine without a full bike licence, but the boy had figured that since he'd not had a valid licence to start with, he'd take the chance of taking it for a blast in the hope that the "friendly" tea-stop cops from Cherry Tree didn't find out - if they had, he could have easily outrun them in their 1300cc *Ford Escort*! The opportunity to take the *Yamaha* for a decent ride had come with the announcement by his older brother that he'd tracked down their father. The kids hadn't seen their Dad since they'd been separated on their initial return from Malta a few years before, and it seemed that he was now living in Norfolk. Ginger's older brother, had by this time, also moved to Lincoln after leaving the maisonette on Albert Square, and the boys had decided to travel to Norfolk – around seventy miles away, on the *Yamaha*. With his brother riding pillion, they'd zoomed off along the flat Lincolnshire roads only for the clutch cable to snap after twenty miles of leaving! Determined to complete the trip and meet their unsuspecting father, Ginger had nursed the big machine along the country roads. As long as they'd not had to stop, the *Yamaha* could be kept bowling along, but without a clutch with which to disengage the engine from the drive chain; stopping for junctions and traffic lights was going to be a problem. Ginger had got around this by slowing down well in advance, dropping the revs to change down a couple of gears and crawling up to the lights in the hope that they'd change to green before they got to them. He'd got it wrong a couple of times and had had to jump the red lights while swerving around other vehicles and watching their irate drivers in his rear view mirrors shaking their fists at the disappearing bike!

The boys had somehow made it unscathed, and limping into the mobile home site where their father lived, they'd dismounted and set about locating the right plot. Walking around the site, they'd spotted him outside his home tinkering with the engine of his car. One of the boys, acting as though they'd just come back from the shops that morning, had said something inane like: 'Hi Dad'. Straightening up from his work and looking up at his now grown-up kids in their motorcycle gear, he'd understandably been at a loss for something to say; after all, its not every day your two sons - lost years before - arrive unannounced on the back of a clapped out old motorcycle! In the end, he'd made do with: 'What are you doing here?' before inviting them inside. In between the long awkward silences, over cups of tea, the father and his sons had slowly reacquainted themselves with one another. They'd not really made much more than small talk and had skirted around the issues of the past. It hadn't been that he hadn't been pleased to see them, but having long since given up on seeing his sons again, it had come as a bit of a shock when they'd turned up out of the blue. After the pain of his family's break up and the years of hurt that had followed, he'd finally been able to put the past behind him and he'd make a new life for himself. The boy's Dad had completed his full term in the RAF before becoming a relief pub landlord and later a school caretaker. During the years that followed their reunion, they'd made the visits more of a regular thing. Sadly, time apart had been time forever lost, and talk of the past; although not totally taboo, had been unwelcome.

Back at Yarborough Road, and within a month of his encounter with the police, the dreaded buff envelope containing the court summons in relation to the boy's heinous crimes had plopped onto the Lion Man's doormat. The bad news had been borne up to the attic room by the Welsh Woman, who had seized upon the tenuous excuse to bore the boy with her and the Lion Man's latest domestic tribulations. Attending court for the first time in his life, the boy had listened while the magistrate had pompously lectured the boy on his wrongdoings and pronounced sentence. He was to be fined eighty pounds – a small fortune in 1978 – and pretty much the same fine a thief might expect to be given in 2012. For good measure, the young motorist had also been given three points on his expired - and so technically non-existent licence.

The boy had discussed his failure to enlist as a Royal Marine with his mentor "R" who'd told him not to worry and had encouraged him to try the army careers office instead. One winter's morning, he'd made his way to Sobraon Barracks on Burton Road, just up from where he lived. The army-recruiting sergeant had, in contrast to his marine counterpart on Saltergate, been far more welcoming. In fact, he'd positively beamed at the prospect of *anyone* walking into his office, and seating the potential recruit down, he'd even gone to the lengths of making him a cup of tea! Putting the army entrance test paper in front of the boy, the sergeant had told him that he had forty minutes in which to complete the questions before, handing him a pencil and eraser, he'd left him to it. Unlike the Royal Marines paper, the maths section had been simplicity itself; presented with basic addition and takeaway problems, even Ginger; whose education had effectively ceased at the age of fourteen, had flown through the section. Next had come a series of multiple-choice questions, apparently relating to reasoning, logic and the English language all rolled into one. One of the actual questions had gone like this:

"Ship is to water, as airplane is to (a) sky (b) road (c) rail

Whizzing through the ridiculously easy test questions in half the allotted time, the boy had sought out the sergeant and declared that he'd completed the paper. A frown of genuine concern had furrowed the sergeant's brow, and reminding him that he still had twenty minutes left in which to finish the test, he'd exhorted the boy to return to his seat and check through his answers! Assuring the man that he had indeed finished, his examiner had checked his answers and within a few minutes, announced that he had passed with flying colours - in fact - with those marks, he could easily apply to be a clerk! The boy had thanked him for the compliment and proudly announced that he'd already decided that he wanted to follow in the footsteps of "R" and join the Royal Regiment of Artillery (He'd quite liked the sound of Germany and all it apparently had to offer!) The sergeant had sent the boy off to the designated army doctor for his entrance medical; the doctor, as luck would have it, had been based on Yarborough Road at a surgery a stone's throw from the Lion Man's house. This had begun to feel like destiny to the boy, who by this time was riding high on the euphoria of actually being valued and wanted for a change. After all the years of rejection and hardship, fate appeared to have dealt him a good hand for a change.

The doctor, who'd been eighty-years old if he'd been a day, had handed the boy a jam jar, minus its original label, and told him unceremoniously to "Piss in that" Satisfying himself that the boy's urine was fit for purpose, the old quack had next instructed his patient to strip and bend over, while he'd peered intently up his backside! Next had come the unfathomable "cough and drop" test, which had required the doctor to cup the boy's balls while telling him to cough. The obligatory eye and hearing test had followed the arse and balls check and the old boy had pronounced the army's latest potential recruit fit to serve his country. Earlier, when he'd been at the barracks and after he'd passed the entry exam, he'd been given a short interview by the sergeant. This had covered all aspects of his current personal life and he had been asked about criminal convictions. The boy had come clean about his moped adventure with the Cherry Tree cops, and explained that he had a fine to pay. The recruiting sergeant had praised the boy's honesty, but impressed upon him, that he was to pay off the eighty pounds fine for his motoring misdemeanours before he would be allowed to enlist in the army. In fact to correctly quote the man with the three stripes on his arm: 'If you go into the army with a fine, they'll chase you from arsehole to breakfast!' The boy hadn't dared to ask who "they" were and didn't exactly relish the thought of "being chased from arsehole to breakfast" – whatever that meant – and so, he'd returned to *Berni's*, properly announced his intended resignation for a change – and strived to pay his fine off as quickly as he could. Working all the overtime he could and paying his fine off in record time, he'd returned to the barracks before the army could change its mind about accepting a boy with no more than two CSE exams to his name and possessing no more than the ability to cook steaks. With head held high, and clutching the sealed envelope containing his medical results, the boy had been sworn into Her Majesty's Armed Forces and been given the modern day's equivalent of his "country's shilling" The traditional shilling - given inflation - had amounted to five pounds and a few odd pence and had been pressed into his hand by the sergeant along with a rail warrant to get him to the army assessment centre in the Midlands town of Sutton Coldfield.

Before he'd left Lincoln, the potential young soldier had climbed the greasy carpeted steps to the tattoo parlour above the George and Dragon public house at the top of Lincoln's High Street. He'd decided to get himself some ink, but this time by a professional - whose eyes looked in the same direction! Back then tattoos had been more common, fashionable even; among those who lived in the north of the country and military men. Following his usual plan of not having a plan, he'd not had a design in mind, but soon after arriving at the parlour, his immature eyes had alighted upon a sample board that had featured a drunken cartoon pink panther holding a bottle of champagne. Telling the uninterested tattooist to put the pink panther onto his right forearm, he'd plonked himself proudly into the dentist-type chair and offered his arm for shaving and disfigurement. It had hurt like hell, but the pain had been more bearable than "J's" handiwork and lessened by the couple of beers he'd consumed on the way there. Paying the princely sum of seven-pounds and fifty pence, he'd left, only to return a few days later to get another one! This time, well and truly hooked by his karate lessons, he'd opted for skull and crossbones wearing a long pigtail tied up in a ribbon and topped off with a straw Chinese coolie hat. Beneath this, he'd asked the tattooist to inscribe the Japanese characters for SKU (*Shukokai Karate Union*) Now the proud owner of tattoos on his right forearm and upper left arm; he'd felt as though he'd completed some kind of rite of passage into manhood. Unfortunately, the artist above the pub had neglected to inform Ginger about tattoo aftercare and when, within a week the tattoos had scabbed over, he'd ignorantly picked at the scabs, eventually leaving patches where the ink had bled out. Once healed, the end result had been a pink panther with no neck and a skull with chunks missing from its pigtail!

Chapter Nine
Boy To Man
'If you can't take a joke, you shouldn't have joined up'

1979, the year that Ginger enlisted, hadn't been one of Britain's finest. The nation's mood had been reflected in chart hits such as Elvis Costello's *"Oliver's Army"*, Pink Floyd's *"Another Brick In The Wall"* and *The Boomtown Rat's "I Don't Like Mondays"* The *Monty Python team's Life Of Brian* blew away the sanctimony of established religion, and Sid Vicious – the self-styled destroyer of the establishment, suffocated on his own vomit and died as a result of a heroin overdose. January saw lorry drivers going on strike, causing shortages of heating oil and fresh food, and tens of thousands of public sector workers went on strike kicking off what would become known as "The winter of discontent" February was memorable for the grave diggers calling off their strike which had left scores of dead unburied, and over 1000 schools were forced to close due to the lack of heating oil caused by the driver's strike. March was no better with Sir Richard Sykes – British ambassador to the Netherlands, being shot dead by the Irish Republican Army in the Hague, and Airey Neave; World War Two veteran and Conservative spokesman for Northern Ireland, was killed by a bomb planted by the Irish National Liberation Army, in the House of Commons car park. In the same month, three years since Ginger had left Malta, the Royal Navy also withdrew from the islands. March had also been the month when the boy; now officially a man, was given a new pair of boots to put on, but this time they laced up, were unyielding and had to be highly polished! By a happy coincidence, 1979 had been the year when Britain had elected its first female prime minister. What had made the very separate events of army enlistment and the election of Margaret Thatcher a happy coincidence, had been the fact that shortly after she took office; she'd given the Armed Forces a staggering 19% pay rise!

Clutching his rail warrant and a small case of belongings, the army's latest potential recruit, had caught a train to Birmingham

New Street station, from whence he'd been instructed to board another, to Sutton Coldfield. There, for the next three days, he was to be assessed both physically and mentally with the intention of placing him with a suitable branch of the army. Arriving at New Street, he'd looked at the numerous bustling platforms and tried to figure out from which one the train to Sutton Coldfield left. Initially, the arrogant pride of youth had prevented him asking for advice, but when after some time, he'd failed to locate the right platform; he'd given in and approached a surly-looking railway guard. Asking the man to point him in the right direction, he'd not been prepared for what had come next. Asking Ginger whether he was joining the army - and receiving the proud answer in the affirmative - the guard had smirked and told him that if that were the case, he would have to: "learn to think for himself" and with that, he'd spun on his heel and walked off chuckling to himself! Ironically, once a soldier, it had been often repeated that he "Wasn't paid to think, only to do!"

Eventually finding the right platform, he'd just about made the next train to leave and had settled down for the short journey to the place that was to shape his destiny for the next three years and beyond.

Along with several other apprehensive young men, he'd been met at the station by a corporal who'd seen them aboard a bus and on their way to the assessment centre. The purpose of the centre at Sutton Coldfield had been to induct potential recruits into the service and determine – with the help of regular soldiers from all branches – just who was suitable for what. They hadn't been that fussy back in the 1970's and providing a recruit was in possession of four limbs and could string a sentence together, he would more than likely make the grade. The newcomers had been issued with the very basics of a uniform – just enough it seemed, to make them feel that they were already soldiers. They had strutted around in bottle-green polyester trousers known as "barrack dress trousers" which in the words of the grinning clothing store man; had: "fitted where they touched," a woolen and very itchy "KF" shirt, a green woollen pullover and a pair of black lace-up plimsoles. If Ginger had thought wearing the uniform had turned him prematurely into a soldier, the bellowing, sarcastic tones of a sergeant soon put paid to this impression. As he'd strolled around Sutton Coldfield camp, hands clasped behind his back, he had been bawled out by the sergeant who had shouted: 'Get your hands from behind your back! Who'd you think you are? Prince fuckin Philip?'

For the physical tests, they'd been issued with white or red v-necked tee shirts and a pair of voluminous dark blue shorts, to be worn with the plimsoles. The fitness tests had been basic at best, with the only requirement being the ability to perform three push-ups, sit-ups and pull-ups. Accustomed to hauling heavy weights back in Malta, lifting homemade barbells and karate training, Ginger had been flabbergasted when he'd witnessed those of his peers who'd been unable to do so much as a single pull-up on the bars. So keen had the army been back then to get hold of as many willing volunteers as they could, the physical training staff at the centre had actually kept the weaklings on for a few extra days and trained them until they had been able to reach the required standard! There had been literally hundreds of potential army recruits at Sutton Coldfield, drawn from all walks of life, and in the evening of his first day there, Ginger had joined the long queue of those old enough to be served at the centre's bar. So long had the queue been and so inefficient were the bar staff, that he'd only been able to buy a couple of beers before the bar had closed. Later, when he'd retired to his designated accommodation block, he'd been just about to doze off into a Lager induced sleep in his dormitory of around a dozen men, when the door to the room had burst open to admit a gang of what could only be described as thugs; intent on bullying those within. Made up of wiry street-wise black kids from North London, razor-scarred Scotsmen and punchy northerners; the gang, united in their common cause of wreaking havoc, had got drunk and gone in search of victims to terrorise. Ginger, quite used to standing up for himself, had ridden out the storm and eventually got a couple of hours sleep before queuing for the washrooms in the morning and carrying out what were to be his first communal ablutions.

Kicking off the military education of their wide-eyed charges as to the way in which to address army sergeants; the old and bold senior NCOs had grimaced before trotting out an age-old adage to all who dared to shorten their esteemed rank and address them as "Sarge" According to them - *There are only two forms of "sarge" – sau-sarge and mas-sarge!* Chuckling at their own joke – no doubt a staple - the sergeants; military moustaches bristling, had put the recruits through their academic paces before delivering salesman-like pitches in an attempt to sway the candidates towards their own home regiments. This had been closely followed with an attempt at dissuading them from signing up with the unit of their rivals. Whether the competitive sergeants had received some kind of bonus for their efforts, Ginger hadn't known, but one thing had been certain; he hadn't intended to be swayed from his choice of his mentor's old regiment – 50 Missile Regt, Royal Artillery, in exotic-sounding Germany. Truth be known, he hadn't really had a clue about his chosen regiment; only that, according to "R" the state sponsored brothels of Dortmund, had been close by! There hadn't appeared to be a "Sarge" representing the Royal Artillery let alone 50 Missile Regiment, but despite pressure to change his mind and join an infantry regiment, Ginger had stuck to his guns - so to speak – and with a sigh, his interviewing officer had marked his papers accordingly. Rubber stamping his immediate future – that of a Gunner (generally shortened on paper to Gnr) with the Royal Artillery in Germany, the officer had shaken Ginger's hand. He'd then been issued with his army service number of 24519646 (mostly quoted as the last four numbers of 9646 for identification). Now an official army recruit, the young Gnr had proudly returned to Lincoln with another rail warrant and a date to attend 17th Training Regiment Royal Artillery at Woolwich, South London, where in 1716, the first two companies of artillery had been formed.

Memories of the Royal Artillery training depot, Woolwich

April 1979, had found Gnr 9646, on a train from Lincoln St Marks, to London Kings Cross, from where he would travel onwards to Woolwich. When he'd first arrived, the troop to which he'd been allocated (Colenso) had been on "build up" - that is to say, that they'd been pretty much left to their own devices. Smoking, joking and drinking beer in the camp's NAAFI bar, they'd enviously watched those recruits already under training as they marched proudly by. Heads held high, chests puffed with pride; their boot heels had crunched in unison across the parade square and the new arrivals had lapped it up. This phony sense of security was to last until such time as the troop would be up to full strength, and with recruits arriving daily from across the UK, this hadn't taken much more than a week. They'd been largely left alone during build up and their bombardier (the Royal Artillery equivalent of a corporal) had displayed a congenial manner that had lulled the recruits even deeper into their sense of security. One person who had made his presence felt had been the camp's provost sergeant. With a nasty looking and deeply pock marked face, he'd been in charge of the guardroom and camp discipline. In a repeat of the Sutton Coldfield "Prince Philip" experience; gunner 9646 had first encountered this very angry man while sauntering across the parade square one morning. His ears had been assailed by the spittle-flecked roar of:

'You lad!'

'Who, me?' he'd innocently asked before beginning to walk towards the now puce faced sergeant who was bellowing that the recruit should "double in!" Not comprehending what "double in" had meant, he'd continued to walk towards him. About to bust a gut, the apoplectic man had indicated that he wanted the brand new gunner to run across the square to him, and so casually jogging over, 9646 came to a very non-military halt and looked innocently up at pock face, who was glowering at him from beneath the mirror-shine of the peak of his cap. The tirade resumed:

'Don't you know you're meant to *march* across the parade square?'

'No'

'No - *what!* 'The provost had yelled.

Hesitantly – 'No…sergeant?'

'No – provost sergeant!' he'd corrected. Once the new gunner had had the chance to explain that he'd only just arrived, the sergeant had softened slightly before sending him on his way making him promise to do his best, but without explaining just how he should march!

Ginger had befriended one of his fellow arrivals – a Welshman (inevitably christened "Taff") who had been a bit older than the rest of them and had at some point been a part time soldier in the Territorial Army. Having previous knowledge in the workings of the military and well versed in the art of "bullshit' (how to spit-shine boots etc) he'd been a handy guy to know. During the build up phase, with time to kill and alcohol flowing freely at the NAAFI, the bullies had come back out of the woodwork and begun to pick on the smaller and younger recruits; some of whom had been on their first trip away from their homes and families. One of these bullies had been a vicious Scotsman who Ginger had first encountered running amok at Sutton Coldfield. Over six feet tall, his muscular body was decorated with an array of razor and hatchet scars; accumulated, it seemed, from the nasty tenements in Glasgow where he'd grown up. Along with a huge lumbering and not very bright Londoner – who by his own admission had spent his pre-army enlistment weekends beating up soldiers – he'd engaged in a game of "toothpaste". This had involved arming themselves with steel capped pickaxe handles and bursting in on some sleepy unfortunate in the dead of night. Laughing like maniacs, they'd yelled 'Toothpaste!' before taking it in turns to thrash the very end of their victim's bed - just inches from his feet. This had had the effect of causing the terrified recruit to draw his legs ever further towards his chin and away from the blows. His body now resembled a tube of toothpaste being rolled up in order to get to the last bit, and this had been how the "game" had got its harmless-sounding name. The Scotsman's accomplice had been more of a gentle giant who hadn't appeared to know his own strength, and when not in the company of the Glaswegian thug, he'd merely satisfied himself with meting out the odd "playful" clout. Playful it may have seemed to him, but if you'd been on the receiving end of one of his massive paws, you'd have known about it! One night, Ginger had returned to his dormitory to find the giant urinating into the comatose Welshman's mouth – talk about extreme bonding!

Once Colenso Troop had reached full strength the nightmare had begun - gone were the friendly smiles of the bombardier, to be replaced with the sadistic grins of one who has total control. The bombardier in charge of Ginger's section had been a diminutive man from somewhere near Newcastle, who'd born a striking resemblance to David Bowie. Always impeccably turned out with his uniform starched to the rigidity of cardboard, he'd had the loudest drill voice in the whole depot. Showing the recruits how to "stand at ease" he'd instructed them that on his command of "Squad" they were to brace up - their bodies were to *grow* he'd said.

'Squad!' A nervous and hesitant rippling movement had followed.

'As you were!' a slumping of relaxing shoulders, before without warning, he would spring a "Squad!" on them again. Satisfied that after an hour of "Squad!" his section could now "brace up", he'd gone on to instruct them in the fine art of "coming to attention"

'Squad! – Squad…Shun!'

This had gone on for the better part of the morning, before finally and grudgingly satisfied with his section's efforts, David Bowie had allowed them to go for a tea break.

From that day on, the recruits – kept awake most of the night polishing anything that didn't move – would be gently woken by the marching relief (a regular soldier, normally a lance-bombardier, who was second in command to the night's guard commander) Having been on duty all night in the guardroom, he'd take great delight in carrying out 5:30 wake-up calls for the exhausted recruits. His favourite method of waking the little darlings, had involved dragging the highly polished metal dustbin from the corridor into the dormitory, where he'd beat it with one of the ubiquitous pickaxe handles. The racket had been unbearable and the sadistic bastard hadn't stopped his onslaught until every bleary-eyed recruit had been seen to put his feet on the floor! Anyone who dared ignore the racket would be dragged outside the block while still sprawled on his mattress, and threatened with a sluicing down from the ice-cold contents of the nearest fire bucket! Breakfast had been at 6:30 – for those fortunate to find the time to eat it – because, at 7:00 the section sergeant and David Bowie would descend upon the recruits to carry out their morning inspection of room, washrooms and lockers. Beds would have to be covered with an orange candlewick counterpane that was to be tucked in around the mattress using "hospital corners" and which had to be pulled so tight, as to be able to bounce a coin on it. At the head of the bed, "bed blocks" would have to be displayed.

These were a kind of a precise, oblong bedding sandwich with the blankets forming the "bread" and the pristine white sheets the "filling". Displayed as a cross section, the blocks had to match specified dimensions, have the two black lines completely centered, and be totally devoid of creases. Any bed block found to be lacking in the laid down specification, would be unraveled before being hurled onto the highly polished floor. To try and avoid this daily heartbreak, most recruits favoured freezing their butts off under the counterpane all night rather than utilise the blankets and sheets with which to ward off the cold night air. In so doing, they'd avoided having to make up the blocks every morning and so have time to actually eat breakfast!

Lockers had to laid out to a specific diagram, with shirts and jackets hung in a certain way and razor-sharp creases all facing the same direction. Socks and woollen gloves were squared off into little cubes using cardboard inserts, and placed either side of PT vests, shorts and pullovers. The vests and other small items of clothing had to be folded over yet more cardboard, leaving only a smooth rounded edge, showing from the locker shelf. White vests were to be sandwiched between red vest and blue shorts mimicking the colours of the Union Jack flag. To achieve this exacting locker layout, recruits had to spend most of the night getting it just right - ironing, dusting and constructing bed blocks. Brass window fitments and washroom pipes were to be polished, and the floor coated with evil smelling yellow wax, ready to be buffed up the next morning by pushing weighted metal "bumpers" over it. Come the daily inspection however, the sergeant and David Bowie would inevitably find fault with something in everyone's locker. The result had been mock anger followed by the contemptuous hurling of immaculate clothing onto the floor. In some cases, the entire locker would be toppled over cascading its contents all over the room! Of course, all this had been designed to keep the recruits up all that night getting their lockers ready for the following morning's onslaught. This had ensured that they hadn't got hardly any sleep before the bin-bashing bastard had joyfully dragged them back to the land of the living at 5:30! Once the room inspections had been carried out, it was the turn of the soldiers themselves to be inspected.

Among the items of kit that the new gunners had been issued with, had been a pair of DMS (Direct Moulded Sole) boots and a beret, which under the tutelage of Taff they'd shrunk to size and moulded into shape by first immersing it in scalding water followed by a dunking in ice-cold water. This process had to be repeated several times before the beret could be placed on the head, shaped accordingly and literally left to dry *in situ*. Consequently, recruits could be seen wandering around the accommodation in various forms of undress with a wet beret perched upon their heads while they went about their business of ironing uniform and adding the finishing touches to their locker layouts. The cap badge – proudly worn by the young gunners, depicted a nine pounder rifled muzzle loader, of around 1871, a rammer used to ram the charge into the muzzle, and to the left, a carriage wheel. *"Ubique"*, surmounting the gun, means *"everywhere"* and the motto below it – *"Quo Fas et Gloria Ducunt"* – *"Where right and glory lead us."* As for the DMS boots, covered as they were with pimply leather; these had to be made perfectly smooth before polish could be applied. Again, Taff had taught them the old sweat's trick of heating up the handle of a spoon with which to burn away the pimples. In order to "bull" the boots, layer upon layer of polish would have to be applied along with spit. To achieve the desired "bulled" effect; hour after mind-numbing hour would have to be spent pushing tiny circles of spit around the surface of the boots using a yellow duster – or "bulling rag" - until they shone like glass.

If during morning inspection, any item of uniform didn't come up to the bombardier's standards, the recruit would be ordered to parade that evening at the guardroom with the offending item of uniform to be shown to the guard commander. The inspecting sergeant or bombardier; bored witless at his post, would relish the chance of brightening up his long duty at the expense of a visiting recruit. He would inevitably find fault with whatever item of uniform the recruit presented and would send him back to improve on it every hour throughout the night, until he was satisfied. On the morning that Ginger had been told to attend show parade with his sub-standard boots, he'd spent the evening furiously bulling them, until they were – in his humble opinion – flawless. Proudly bounding over to the guardroom, shiny boots in hand, he'd presented them to the guard commander who was waiting at the window. Without even looking at the shiny uppers he had turned them upside down and inspected the soles. As he'd gleefully suspected, the young gunner hadn't even thought about bulling the bottoms of his boots and without a word, he'd hurled them out of the window! Impacting cruelly with the tarmac, Ginger's boots had bounced miserably along the ground before coming to a halt, battered and scuffed. With the layers of brittle polish now detached from the leather - they'd looked as though they'd been run over by a truck! Picking them up – another lesson learned - he'd walked dejectedly back to the block to start all over again with the guard commander's shout of 'See you in an hour' ringing in his ears. The whole regime had been designed to get the recruits to pull together and hate a common enemy – the instructors.

The sections had taken it in turns to be introduced to the military bread and butter task of guard duty. The guard had consisted of seven gunners overseen by an orderly officer, the sergeant guard commander and a bombardier marching relief (affectionately known as the "marching tealeaf") The guard's duties had been to provide a roving foot patrol and static sentry posts at the front gate to the barracks and also at an arch at the far end of the camp known as Queen's Arch. Below the arch were housed regular female soldiers – known as WRAC's. Shortened from the Women's Royal Army Corps, the women had discouraged the abbreviated version of their Corps saying that, a (W)rac was something to be screwed up against a wall! Queen's Arch, had naturally been a sought after post given its excellent view of the basement accommodation of the WRAC quarters. Peering into those rooms with undrawn curtains, the hormonal, sex-starved teenagers would sometimes be treated to a fleeting glimpse of a WRAC in her underwear before she'd indignantly yanked the curtains closed! Once the peep show had ended, so had the fascination with guard duty at Queen's Arch, and the gunners had resumed their uneventful patrolling. Having not yet been instructed in bearing arms - or trusted enough to carry them, they'd been issued with pickaxe handles with which to protect themselves while on patrol. The gunners had patrolled in pairs and were given a radio with which to communicate with the guardroom. Although the rudimentaries of the radios had been explained, the recruits had yet to be schooled in the complexities of military radio voice procedure and as a hilarious result, they'd answered transmissions from the guardroom, as though making a telephone call, with such inanities as:

'Hello – is that you bombardier?'

The 1970's had been dangerous times to be a soldier; what with the IRA constantly striving to achieve a "spectacular" (Woolwich Barracks would later be bombed by them while the boy's younger brother had been training there). Luckily however, the recruits, armed with nothing more than their pickaxe handles and the bliss of ignorance, had been unaware of the dangers. One particularly humorous marching tealeaf had instructed the rookie guards in the use of their "weapons". They were, he said, to sneak up on amorous couples returning from a night out and copulating in the shelter of the bicycle sheds. He'd told them, with a wicked grin, that they should wait until the "vinegar" stroke before tapping the unsuspecting lovers on the shoulder with their pickaxe handles!

Although the number of gunners required for guard duty was been seven, it has long been military practice to parade an extra man. The eighth and surplus gunner was there to provide an opportunity for all the guard to be awarded what had been known as "stick man" In effect, the extra man was to provide an incentive for all the soldiers to turn out for guard duty impeccably dressed, with combat fatigues crisply starched, and boots "bulled" until they reflected like mirrors. Upon a minute inspection of the men, the orderly officer would nominate the smartest soldier as stick man and dismiss him from guard duty. The lucky man would then be sent back to the block where he'd be given the night off - with the proviso - that should he be required at some point in the night due to another's sickness etc, he was to return to the guardroom for duty. Parade and inspection of the guard, had been generally held on the parade square, but should it have been raining they would assemble in one of the large drill sheds. The sheds had also been occupied by a colony of pigeons that, prior to the advent of the plastic anti-bird spikes common today, had thrived unhindered among the dry haven of the steel rafters. One particular evening as Ginger and seven of his fellow recruits had gathered for the mounting of the nightly guard, they'd looked in envy at one of their number who, without doubt, would be awarded stick man. Creases like razor blades and with so much starch on his uniform that it could have stood up by itself, the potential stick man wore boots that had been subject to hours of bulling. The jet-black polish flaking and cracking with his every step, he'd stood there with the smug look that had said: '*Fuck you boys; I'm getting the night off!*' Just as the orderly officer approached to begin his inspection, one of the drill shed's resident pigeons; disturbed by the loud words of command issued by the guard commander bringing the guard to attention, had let loose the biggest stream of white watery crap, dumping it all over the potential stick man! There had been hardly any part of his painstakingly starched uniform that had escaped the results of the bird's startled dump! The guard commander; who'd only minutes earlier, congratulated the man on his appearance, virtually tipping him for stick man, roared that the unfortunate and fidgeting man should: "keep bloody still", before marching up to the orderly officer and handing over the inspection. Reaching the crap-covered soldier, the orderly officer had made some remark about the smell before sending him off to get cleaned up and awarding the prestigious stick man to someone else!

After a couple of weeks of barrack routine, the new gunners had been taken out on their first field exercise. These exercises were held not far from the camp on military estate known as Pit Park. Sparsely wooded and muddy, Pit Park had been riddled with half-dug holes, hurriedly filled-in trenches and stagnant ponds. The recruits would be taken to the park for a period of 48 hours, during which they'd learn all about field craft, camouflage and different methods of patrol. They would also be given demonstrations of, among other things, how noise and light carried at night. The recruits would be introduced to army ration packs and educated in the art of cooking them over hexamine stoves, before being split into groups of three and sent off to dig trenches. Once the new soldiers had dug their holes and fed themselves, they had been instructed to put out sentries and make themselves comfortable for the night - that is to say - as comfortable as was possible in the depths of a muddy trench during a wet English spring. When not on sentry duty, the soldiers had been told to get some sleep. What the kids hadn't known, was that sleep for the recruits during the 48 hours that were to follow, hadn't been part of the instructor's plans; the opposite in fact was to be the case. The idea had been to put the fledgling gunners under as much stress as was possible to see how they coped, and so waiting until the unsuspecting recruits had dug their trenches, cooked a meal and settled down for the night, they'd run through the trench lines throwing "thunderflashes" (which simulated grenades) among the startled kids. Screaming at them to "bug out" of their positions, they had run them around the park leaving a trail of mess tins, sleeping bags, groundsheets and rations in their wake. Disorientated and in total darkness the bewildered recruits had been assembled and then instructed to start over and dig fresh trenches. This had gone on all night with the instructor's attacks growing in intensity until at 3am, dog tired, wet, muddy and cold, Ginger and his comrades had resolved not to dig another trench or to climb into their sleeping bags – after all, what would have been the point? they'd only have to vacate it within the next hour or so! Instead, they'd placed a groundsheet on the muddy ground and joined the remaining two sheets together with the brass poppers, before lying their filthy, weary bodies down and pulling the doubled up sheets over themselves. In the event, the recruits hadn't been attacked again that night and three hours of violent shivering later, they'd been woken up for the day's instruction, before which - and before breakfast, they had to return to all the trenches they'd abandoned during the night and fill them back in.

After breakfast and a wash and shave in cold water, the gunners had been taken to a clearing in the woods where a flatbed lorry had been converted into a makeshift stage. With the intention of restoring morale after such a wretched night, the instructors, in the age-old army tradition, had arranged for the sections to compete with one another and put on skits. These generally took the form of parodying officers and instructors, but any kind of entertainment, such as song and dance routines or stand up comedy, was encouraged. The instructors had gamely joined in with the skits with a memorable performance by a bombardier and his cohorts. The bombardier had been introduced to his audience of sleep-deprived gunners in the style of a boxing MC by a sergeant, as: the undefeated "spoon-bashing" champion of Woolwich. Meanwhile, two chairs were set up at opposite ends to a small table and occupied by the bombardier and one of his mates. The two soldiers had then been blindfolded and the handles of dessertspoons placed between their teeth. The object of the game had been for the contestants to take it in turns to hit one another over the head with the spoons. As one may imagine, not a great deal of power can be exerted using ones mouth and so, to the watching recruits, it hadn't seemed such a great deal and they'd been surprised, when after three or four lame looking blows from the champion, his opposite number had capitulated. Stepping back up on stage, the sergeant MC had built the whole thing up asking whether there had been anyone in the audience who thought they could take the champion bombardier on at spoon bashing. One of the lads, who'd fancied himself as a bit of a hard man, had stepped forward and been duly ushered with much ceremony onto the stage. Blindfold applied, he'd taken the seat opposite the champ and been invited by the MC to land the first hit. Leaning forward, he'd brought the spoon down onto the head of the bombardier, delivered a fairly respectable blow and been cheered by the assembled recruits. Now it had been the turn of the champ, and entering stage left had been the troop commander with a huge soup ladle in his hand. Putting his finger to his lips, the MC had demanded silence from his audience before asking the volunteer hard man whether he was ready to be struck by the champ. Receiving a fairly scornful 'yes' in reply, The MC nodded to the troop commander and stood back to enjoy the spectacle. Raising the soup ladle about a foot above the kid's head, the troop commander had brought it crashing down onto his skull! Reeling under the blow, the kid had stubbornly shaken off the chance to resign and had delivered another weak blow to the champ's head. Asking him if he was ready to be hit with the return blow, he'd answered – with slightly less conviction than before – that he was. Another cracking rap over the head with the TC's soup ladle had forced submission and he'd groggily removed his blindfold to howls of laughter from his companions and the sight of the officer brandishing the ladle! Both the spoon bashing victim and the rest of Colenso Troop had learned a valuable lesson that day – don't *ever* volunteer for *anything* in the army!

Once a week, the recruits had to attend "pay parade" They'd been given a weekly allowance of twenty pounds with the remainder of their pay put into savings until the end of their training, which had given them a tidy sum with which to enjoy post-training leave. Pay parade had involved marching up to the troop commander, smartly halting in front of him before saluting, and being handed a brown envelope containing twenty pounds. The march up, halt and subsequent salute had to be perfect, or else the recruit would be sent back to the end of the line to repeat the procedure until it was performed to the officer's satisfaction. Even those deemed worthy of receiving their pay would march up to the officer, salute and have the pay packet contemptuously dropped to the floor before it could be taken from the officer's hand. This had obliged the recruit to forgo any remaining dignity and scrabble around on the floor to retrieve it. These were the typical actions of a jumped-up upper class twit of an officer, and similarities were to be witnessed more than once in Ginger's army career. When it had been his turn to march up and collect his twenty pounds, Ginger – not the best participant at drill at the best of times – had failed to impress the snotty TC and had barely got within six feet of him, when the Troop Commander had glanced meaningly at the troop sergeant, who'd yelled at him to "Get in the fuckin bin!" Getting hold of the hapless recruit and dragging him along the polished corridor, he'd unceremoniously dumped him onto the floor next to the same bin that the marching tealeaf had bashed each morning, and ordered that he get in! Climbing miserably into the dustbin, Ginger had looked up too late to prevent the heavy metal lid being dropped from arm's length onto his head. Dazed and literally seeing stars, he'd been ordered to chant: 'I am rubbish!' He'd had to constantly chant the self-insulting mantra until another unfortunate had been sent to replace him! Once the instructors had grown bored with the bin game, and all the recruits had been in receipt of their twenty pounds, they would be marched to the NAAFI shop and made to spend at least half of it on starch, polish and dusters!

Pay parade hadn't been the only form of humiliation that the recruits had been subjected to either; every day, at the end of training, the instructors would wait until the gunners had been taking a shower before dishing out the mail. Being away from home, the arrival of a letter was something of a morale booster for the trainees, and armed with this knowledge, the sergeants and bombardiers would stand at the end of the corridor, shouting out the names of those recruits lucky enough to have mail. Cruelly playing on the kid's eagerness to get a letter, they'd command the gunners to sprint along the corridor to collect their post. One evening, Ginger had been in the shower, when a fellow recruit had come in to say that the sergeant had called his name for mail. Not having any family to speak of, this had been a rare event and he'd been quite excited. Covered in soap and dripping wet, he'd put his head around the washroom door and told the sergeant that he'd be out as soon as he'd showered. 'If you don't come right now', he'd been gruffly told, 'your letter will go in the bin!' Slipping and sliding naked along the polished corridor, he'd gone to receive his mail only to find that rather than a standard letter; it was in fact, a telegram. Back then, in the days before mobile phones and text messages, the telegram had been the only form of instant messaging available and what was more, telegrams only tended to be sent in times of emergency such as to announce death or grave illness. Puzzled, he'd taken the telegram from the sergeant, who'd insisted that he open it in his presence in case it was truly an emergency that would have necessitated his interaction with the kid. Concern soon turned into grudging admiration when the content of the "urgent" telegram was revealed to contain nothing sinister at all. In fact bizarrely, it had been sent by no other than "G" the barmaid at *Berni's*, declaring her undying love! Ginger had added it to the last item she'd sent him – a 45 inch vinyl of *"Rikki don't lose that number"* by *Steely Dan*. "G" had crossed out the name *Rikki* and above it, in her unmistakable writing, she'd written his name instead!

As training had progressed, the recruits had undergone small arms training and for the first time, been issued with the menacing looking L1A1 self-loading rifle. Introduced in 1954 as a British derivative of the Belgian FN FAL battle rifle, it originally came encased in walnut furniture, with later models in black plastic. Fitted with a magazine that held twenty 7.62mm rounds, its muzzle velocity was 2,700 feet per second. Placing such a devastating weapon into young hands had demanded hours of deadly serious skill at arms lessons, and after 10 weeks of basic training, the recruits had been able to list each and every part of the rifle and strip and assemble it blindfolded and deal with any stoppages. Once they'd been trusted to fire the SLR, the recruits had trooped down to the live firing range where, under the watchful eyes of the instructors, they put the lessons of marksmanship principles into practice and undertaken the mandatory annual personal weapons test (APWT) If you didn't treat the SLR with respect it would bite – too loose a hold meant at best a punishing hammer blow on the shoulder, and at worst a fractured cheek bone and possible loss of teeth! If the recruits neglected to wear the cheap plastic ear- plugs, their ears would ring painfully for the rest of the day, (although Ginger had seen one resourceful kid stuffing cigarette filters into his ear drums to replace his lost plastic plugs!). Lying down too closely to a fellow recruit on the firing point also hadn't been advisable – red hot ejected cartridge cases have a tendency to fly out of the rifle when fired, and deposit themselves painfully down the backs of loose fitting jackets. Range discipline being what it is, means that rolling around in a demented attempt to free the searing brass case, while holding a loaded rifle of your own, just isn't an option! Taff had taught them the trick of firing at the gravel in front of the targets to kick up tiny stones that would in turn hit the target and make it fall. (The electronically operated targets would fall when hit and so register a score) Employing the Welshman's advice, Ginger had scraped through the APWT, but not come anywhere near winning the coveted cloth badge of crossed rifles that was awarded to those few recruits who excelled at shooting. Those that had would be permitted to sew the crossed rifles onto their uniform sleeves, denoting them as a Marksman. The SLR had become an extension of the recruit's bodies; hours of small arms training and similar hours of parade practice involving foot drill; which had begun to incorporate rifle drill, had made the young gunners feel as though something had been missing after they'd handed their rifles into the armoury at the end of the day.

Deemed proficient and safe enough to leave camp and go out into the big wide world with their SLRs, the new gunners had been bussed out to the live firing ranges at Hythe in Kent. There, they were to spend a few days slogging their way around march-and-shoot courses, with a little parade practice thrown in at night. The accommodation had been spartan, but the instructors had relaxed the regime of locker layout inspections, concentrating instead on

147

the recruit's fitness, shooting and the ongoing weeding out of those who in the long run, hadn't really been suited to soldiering. The troop had already lost around a quarter of its strength, with those *Walter Mitty's* who'd enlisted with ideas of jumping out of airplanes and storming machine gun nests while clasping a bayonet between their teeth, being shown the door. They'd quickly cracked under the strain of late nights, early mornings, constant inspections and group interaction. Hythe was to take its toll on the remaining dreamers, with its emphasis on grueling speed marches loaded down with kit, and team exercises. On the first evening at Hythe, the gym instructors had assembled the gunners in the gymnasium where they had arranged long wooden gym benches to form a square. Roughly pairing the recruits by their height, they'd thrown a pair of heavy boxing gloves at them before setting the pairs up against each other to "mill" Milling had been the old military name for fist fighting or boxing, and with no regard given to previous boxing experience, the gunners had gone at it hammer and tongs. It wasn't important who won, it had just been the instructor's way of fostering team spirit and testing levels of aggression within a controlled environment. There had only been one refusal – some joker who'd talked a good fight, but hadn't the guts to slog it out toe to toe with his comrades. Using the bizarre excuse that it had been "against his religion" to fight, he'd been told to pack his kit and had been gone within the hour. Nobody ever discovered which religion he'd subscribed to, but upon returning to Woolwich, the refusenik had been discharged from the army. Ginger had been lucky enough not to have been paired with an experienced boxer and had acquitted himself well. The twit of a troop commander – assuming that his spiky hair meant he was a punk – had shouted encouragement: 'Come on punk rocker!'

Returning from Hythe, the gunners had been a tight team and had begun to take pride in their troop. A certain amount of rivalry had existed between the training troops but as far as Ginger's lot had been concerned, Colenso was the best. This had been reflected in the songs they'd sung as they marched through camp, heads held high and chests swollen with pride:

'Everywhere we go-oh
People ask us
Who we are-r

So we tell them
  We are Colenso – mighty, mighty Colenso
  And if they don't hear us…
  We shout a bit louder
  And if they don't hear us…
  They must be deaf!'

The sergeants and bombardiers, by creating a common enemy out of themselves, had, it seemed, done their job well. Now all that remained was to get their charges parade perfect and ready for the final passing out parade, which concluded ten weeks of basic training. After passing out, they would be handed over to their gunnery instructors for the four weeks of gunnery training that would finally entitle the recruits to call themselves gunners in the Royal Regiment of Artillery.

It had to be said, that Ginger and drill hadn't been a marriage made in heaven and when after being drilled for the entire morning, his leg had begun to visibly tremble with the strain of remaining to attention for so long, sergeant "C" had shouted;

'Oi! Elvis fuckin Presley! Stand still!'

They'd spent hours perfecting rifle drill and executing complicated movements such as "grounding arms" This drill movement had involved the simultaneous laying down of their SLRs onto the tarmac, before at a signal from the bombardier, rising as one and marching away from their rifles. After a lap around the parade ground, they'd march back onto the rifles and as one, pick them up and return them to the shouldered position. As the final parade had got nearer, the rifles had been fitted with gleaming chromed bayonets. They'd carried out rifle drill leaving the scabbards attached, but come the big day, they would be removed and the wicked blades would be on show. The recruits had now begun to rehearse their final parade with the band and they'd felt ten feet tall. The pass out parade was to be a grand affair with family and friends invited, stirring speeches made by the officers and plenty of pompous martial music followed by a buffet get-together for the soldiers and their guests. Ginger had been a little disappointed at having nobody to come and witness his transition from boy to man and when he'd mentioned it to sergeant "C", the NCO had feigned sympathy, before telling him that he would bring his daughter to be Ginger's guest. Eyes lighting up at the prospect of a female coming to witness his big day, he'd wondered what she would look like. The grizzled sergeant had, as an apparent afterthought dashed any notion the recruit may have been harbouring in relation to his daughter, when laughing, he'd continued – 'Yes, she's six years old – now fuck off and stop whining!'

On the final parade, two recruits had fainted – either because of drinking the night before, or due to the length of time they'd been standing to attention. The first had fallen backwards, narrowly avoiding being impaled on the gleaming bayonet of a soldier in the rear rank. Under strict instructions not to move regardless of what happened, the gunners had stood stock-still. Ginger hadn't been far off collapsing either, but his comrade fainting had had the psychological effect of stiffening his resolve not to be next! Once the parade ended, the soldiers had literally marched across the comatose soldier as if he hadn't been there, and later while in the NAAFI, the relatives of the unfortunate man had been assured that the gunner was fine and had made a full recovery!

After four weeks of training on the 105mm light gun and a final firing exercise on Salisbury Plain, Ginger had made the grade and officially become a gunner. He'd gone back to Woolwich to discuss his posting and had been disappointed to learn that his request to join 50 Missile Regiment had been turned down due to an issue with his security vetting. 50 Missile, being a nuclear-capable regiment, had strict vetting procedures in place, and upon discussion with a sergeant, he'd come to the conclusion, that as he had a half brother still living in Malta (the government of which was still cosying up to Libya and the Chinese) he'd possibly been turned down for the regiment of his choice because of the potential "by proxy" threat. That was to say, that should his brother in Malta be leant upon to illicit sensitive information from his soldier brother, military confidentiality may have been at risk of being breached. Salesman-like, the sergeant had trumpeted the virtues of various other choices of regiment among which had been Twenty-Second Air Defence Regiment. 22A/D had progressed from 40/70 *Bofors* anti-aircraft guns and were now equipped with the exciting (but technically rubbish) Rapier anti-aircraft missile system. This radar enabled missile launcher, had been intended as a medium level weapon with an effective ceiling of 10,000 feet and when it worked – which was seldom – it had been impressive. The problem had been, that Rapier, designed for static airfield defence, hadn't fared well when dragged across muddy and rutted German fields in the hands of the army. It had simply been too delicate and three years after he'd left Woolwich, during the battle to retake the Falklands, Rapier was to be exposed as extremely lacking in effectiveness. Once Ginger had discovered that 22A/D were based not only in Germany; but also shared the town of Dortmund with the brothel he'd heard so much about from "R" at *Berni's*, 50 Missile was forgotten about and his German adventure had been on the brink of beginning…

Going back to Lincoln to await a posting date, he'd proudly worn the black and yellow Colenso Troop sweatshirt and strutted along the High Street until he'd been stopped by an elderly lady who'd asked him if he were in the army! That had made his day; at last he'd felt as though he belonged, was important. Beaming at the woman, he'd replied that: 'yes he was!' 22A/D's latest recruit had spent two weeks on leave during which he'd put a sizeable dent in the fourteen weeks' worth of pay put aside for him by the instructors back in Woolwich. He'd even re-acquainted himself with "G" of telegram-sending fame!

Making his way to the Bedfordshire airport of Luton, Ginger caught the air trooping flight to Dusseldorf and after a short flight, boarded a military coach to Dortmund. He'd been met at the gates to Napier Barracks by the battery runner - aka the battery rabbit – who had been tasked with showing the rookie around the massive camp that had formerly been the wartime home to the German Luftwaffe. The newly- arrived gunner had been assigned to 11 (Sphinx) Battery and after being shown around camp, he'd attended the Regimental Restaurant - known colloquially by the troops as the "cookhouse". It had been there, that his feeling of belonging and self-importance had been dealt a humiliating blow. The regiment had consisted of three missile batteries; numbered and named after past battle honours - 42 (Alem Hamza) 53 (Louisburg) and 11 (Sphinx) The batteries had been supported practically by Headquarter Battery; which provided drivers, cooks, clerks and so forth, and technically, by the Royal Electrical and Mechanical engineers (REME) The latter provided technicians to nurse the useless Rapier, and mechanics to keep the regiment's fleet of Landrovers and heavy goods vehicles on the road. There had also been a contingent from the Royal Army Ordnance Corps (RAOC), whose role had been that of weapons and ammunition supply, weapon maintenance and general supply.

Within the cookhouse, unbeknown to Ginger, there had been a kind of unwritten etiquette with regard to who sat where and with whom. Invisible lines had been drawn up and one didn't sit down to eat at a table occupied by members of a rival battery. This had been more prevalent among the missile batteries than the support troops and had extended to off duty drinking, where certain bars, adopted by the various batteries, would be off limits to their rivals. The only exception to the rule had been strictly by invitation only. The new gunner had selected a table with two or three men already seated at it and sat down with his food. He'd smiled nervously at the men who'd eyed him with suspicion, before one of their number; a fiery redheaded man ("R") had asked him if he were a member of 53 Battery. When he'd replied that he wasn't, "R" had told him to: 'Fuck off then!' Picking up his tray, the crestfallen and red-faced new arrival had sought out a table that had been unoccupied, and miserably eaten his dinner. That night he'd spent an uneasy night in an old accommodation block known as Block 77. Run down and looking rather dirty and makeshift, it had echoed with the sounds of drunken men coming and going throughout the night. Things were thrown around and abuse hurled. It had seemed a lot like the block in Sutton Coldfield and Ginger had felt isolated and not a little concerned. What he hadn't known was that Block 77 had also been home to the battery bar, where off duty soldiers would spend a few hours getting tanked up on cheap beer before heading out to the local Dortmund bars, where they would often drink steadily into the early hours regardless of the fact that they had to start work at 08:00.

The next morning, groggy from lack of sleep, 22 A/D's latest member, had been introduced to a diminutive and skinny officer who was Troop Commander for Delta Troop, into which he was to be inducted. Second Lieutenant "J" didn't look a day over 19 and spoke with the clipped upper-class tones of one born into privilege. He'd seemed decent enough though, and had been civil enough to the new kid, even offering him a cigarette from a fancy silver case before giving him an ineffectual but welcoming pep talk. He'd then been sent to the battery lines, which in effect, were a series of four garages (one per troop). It had taken him all morning to get around to being introduced to his new boss; in part because nobody knew, or was prepared to enlighten him as to where he was actually to go. As a result, he'd been passed around from garage to garage where he was given odd jobs to do by all and sundry until around lunch time, when he'd finally made it to the end garage - home to D Troop. There he'd been met by a barrel-chested sergeant; arms covered with tattoos and with the bottom half of his face almost obscured by a magnificent bushy moustache. Sergeant Johnny Cookson (RIP) the detachment commander of Bravo sub- detachment, stroking his luxuriant whiskers; had patiently listened to Ginger's excuse for not having presented himself sooner, before uttering his trademark catchphrase of: 'If you can't take a joke, you shouldn't have joined up!' He'd then put him to work painting vehicles - along with road sweeping, the most common peacetime pastime - and with that, he'd embarked upon the first of two periods of army service...

Incidentally, a year or so after arriving in Dortmund, the now established Gnr, had once again encountered the scarred bully of a Glaswegian. He'd had cause to visit 26 Field Regiment – which had also been based in Dortmund, and in the guardroom, awaiting transport to Colchester military prison (Military Correctional Training Centre), had been the "toothpaste tormentor" The system it seemed, had finally caught up with the nasty bastard and put him behind bars where he undoubtedly belonged!

Postscript
'I'm sorry…'

May 1996 – 21 years after leaving Malta.

Twenty-one years older and an interesting and varied life
behind me, I had been working as a residential social worker in the
market town of Aylesbury, Buckinghamshire, when I received
word from my brother that the man – ogre of 41 Valletta Road –
was on his deathbed. My brother, who unlike me, and to my
shame, had been in more regular contact with my half-brother
back in Malta; had been told that his father had been the victim of
a stroke and that he wasn't expected to live much longer.
Throughout my adult life, up to the point of learning of the man's
imminent demise, I'd stubbornly refused to acknowledge the
reasons for my sometimes-erratic behaviour. I'd not bothered to
seek the root cause of the recurring nightmares and the dark and
angry mood swings, visited upon long-suffering loved-ones. I'd
not once attempted to analyse my propensity for explosive
violence and the inability to sleep through the night. In all the
years since running away from number 41 Valletta Road, I'd never
returned to the island where my mother lay under the arid earth
and my half-brother lived in the semi-isolation of being neither
British nor Maltese. It wasn't until I'd been in receipt of the news
from Malta, and with a child of my own, that I had resolved to face
my demons head on. I reasoned that I would never find closure
once the man had passed away, and taking leave from my work, I
traveled to Malta within the week. In my work of semi-fiction, ***By
Conscience Bound***, I wrote about my trip to Malta and subsequent
visit to the man who used to drive the Chevy Impala. My account
is true to most events, but here is what actually happened…

    I had re-established contact with my half-brother and informed
him of my intention to visit Malta. Having been little more than a
baby when I'd broken my promise to my dying mother and left
him behind, he'd no real inkling of the hardship his mother and
siblings had faced under the tyranny of his father. Consequently,
when I touched down at Luqa Airport after many years, he'd
kindly come to collect me and put himself at my disposal. He

confirmed that his father had indeed suffered a stroke and that despite some mental peculiarities; he'd remained *compos mentis*. Due to the stroke having affected his mobility, he had been put in to a nursing home a short distance from Luqa and the following morning my brother picked me up and took me to visit him. As I've already mentioned, my brother, through no fault of his own, had been oblivious to most of what had gone on during those dark days at number 41, and as we drove to the nursing home, he had an air of excitement about him. It appeared that as far as he was concerned, this was to be a happy reunion, the return of the prodigal son almost. I didn't shatter his illusions and the last thing that I had wanted was a confrontation; it had just been something that I instinctively knew I needed to do. I had to exorcise my Maltese past and banish forever the barely beneath the surface anger and sorrow of those 21 years past.

Arriving at the nursing home, I followed my brother into the gloom of the ward and listened as he announced to his father that he had: "a surprise for him" And there he was: propped up by pillows and dressed in faded white and blue pyjamas with the crusty remains of that morning's breakfast spilled down the front of his top. He looked older of course, but looking into those rheumy eyes, I could still see the latent malevolence. He looked at me, his pathetic stroke-ridden body attempting to move, but managing no more than a squirming shuffling motion. My brother helped him to sit up and repositioned the pillows. I looked down at him; the empty husk on the bed with food all down his front no longer generated fear. Those useless limbs would never be capable of kicking, slapping or punching me again. I don't know why I did it – maybe because I'd wanted to fully exorcise my ghosts – but reaching down, I actually took the old man's gnarled hand in mine, holding on to it for a while. Perhaps it had been the indirect connection to my mother; I really don't know; it certainly hadn't been out of affection! The first thing that the man said to me was: 'I'm sorry…' His voice trailed off and I actually thought the old bastard was apologising to me! My illusions were corrected when he continued: 'That because I'm here, I cant look after you like I used to' Suppressing a laugh, I remember thinking to myself that thank God he *couldn't* look after me like he used to! He then went on to talk about the past and with a smile, recalled how he had given us so-called *pet* names – *mouse, pig, scissors* etc. I was flabbergasted; he was actually remembering those insulting names with fondness, like we'd enjoyed his stupid nicknames! He also told me that he hadn't wanted me to leave in the first place, but I just didn't think it had been appropriate to discuss my flight from the island. Harking back to his belief in all things British and the mumbo jumbo of the *Man, Myth Magic* magazines, he'd asked me whether when I got back to the UK, I could seek out publications, which could somehow teach him to beat his stroke. He went on to boast about how he'd gone from smoking forty cigarettes a day before his stroke, to not smoking at all. He had, he claimed, given up overnight. I hadn't the heart to tell him that having a stroke will do that to a man! I will admit that walking out of that gloomy ward and into the brilliant sunshine, I did feel as though a weight had been lifted from me, and all it had taken had been for me to clap eyes on the man who'd made me so miserable, hungry and at times suicidal.

Dutifully looking after me during my visit, my brother drove me around the island on a bit of a "for old times sight-seeing tour" and on the way to his house – still under construction – he showed me something that stopped me in my tracks. On the way to his house, he stopped at a spot overlooking the Blue Grotto. This is a popular tourist haunt famous for the unusual hue of the sea. In effect, it is a collection of caverns, the location of which, combined with sunlight, leads to the water mirroring and showing numerous shades of blue. Several of the caves mirror the phosphorescent colours of the underwater flora. So striking is the Blue Grotto that it was chosen for a scene in the film *Troy* starring Brad Pitt. But I digress! My brother had stopped, so that he could show me the scene of an accident. There, on a winding stretch of road close to a steel road barrier, he bade me to get out of the car and continue on foot. We hopped over the barrier and walked a few yards across a plateau, which, after a few more feet, had become a sheer drop down the cliff face into the glittering azure sea below. My brother, at this point, had had no idea that I'd written **By Conscience Bound**, which, I'd loosely based on the promise I'd made to my mother with regard to looking after him. Actually, it had yet to be published and had been more of a cathartic project rather than the beginning of a writing career.

Walking across the plateau, no more than a few feet from the edge of the cliff, he showed me pieces of car wreckage, faded and bleached by the sun of several summers.

What had stopped me dead had been his explanation of how the wreckage had come to be there; it had been the wreckage of *his* car. At around the time when he'd gone sailing through the crash barrier - his flip-flops caught under the brake pedal - I'd been midway through writing **By Conscience Bound** - which for those still to read it, I won't spoil the story. Suffice to say, he'd been involved in an almost identical accident to that which I'd described happening to his character in my book! I didn't mention this to him, as I'd felt bad enough leaving him behind all those years ago - let alone writing him into a real life near-fatal accident!

Later, I went with my brother to visit his other parent – my mother. He proudly showed me a beautiful headstone that after twenty-odd years, he and his father – ever the craftsman – had fashioned from local stone. Before this, there had only been the faded etchings of the Ginger Lady, who'd marked the occasion of my mother's death with her door key. Set in the headstone – topped with a carved stone crucifix - is a marble plaque bearing her name and date of her death. Above the inscription, my brother and his father had affixed a photograph immortalised on ceramic plate. It's a beautiful image of my mother; taken while on a beach back in the salad days of her blossoming romance with the man and I love it for its non-conformity among the formal graveyard pictures of long-dead people surrounding her - all traditionally depicted in their Sunday best clothes. With her rebellious nature she'd have appreciated it too and I genuinely thank my brother and his father for erecting such a fitting memorial to her. I still visit the island whenever I can now that the demons have been banished, and I have discovered that Antonia; (the Ginger Lady), whose family, I believe to be in Australia, has been laid to rest (at her request) alongside my mother. Whenever I visit the cemetery, I take my mum's favourite *Cala* lilies to put on her grave and while I pull at the weeds and talk to her about what I've been up to since my last visit, I can't help but shed a few tears for the mother I have long since outlived and who will never again regale me with stories of the bear who loved *Fry's Chocolate Cream*.

To be continued…

VM Frost
London, September 2012

Made in the USA
Charleston, SC
15 February 2013